God's Wisdom
For
a Fair and Just
World

Dr. Jim Richards

True Potential
REACH THE WORLD

God's Wisdom For a Fair and Just World

Cover and Interior Page design by True Potential, Inc.

ISBN: (Paperback): 9781953247063

ISBN: (e-book): 9781953247070

True Potential, Inc.

PO Box 904, Travelers Rest, SC 29690

www.truepotentialmedia.com

Produced and Printed in the United States of America.

Contents

Why I Wrote This Book   5
1. The Outrage of the World   7
2. How Did We Get Here?   10
3. The Lie We All Believe   14
4. Identifying the Real Enemy   17
5. Why We Don't Want to Perceive   23
6. Can We Read and Understand the Signs?   27
7. Wars and Rumors of Wars   30
8. Do Not Become Troubled   33
9. Nation Will Rise Against Nation   37
10. Cultivating Ethnic Warfare   40
11. Creating A World of Victims   46
12. Racism   50
13. The Great Shaking   55
14. Pandemics, Healthcare, and Total Control   57
15. The Beginning of Sorrows   62
16. Giving Birth to What?   65
17. What You See Isn't Always What You Perceive   68
18. The Mystery of Lawlessness   72
19. The Power of Godly Influence   78
20. The Process and the Promise   83
21. Harmonizing Heaven and Earth   86
22. Compassion that Kills or Heals   90
23. The Justice of God or The Justice of Man   95
24. The Penalty Must Match the Offense   100
25. Is Man More Righteous than God?   104
26. Gathering or Scattering   107

Share this important message with your family, friends, church and community.

Use your smartphone camera on the flowcode images below to share *God's Wisdom for a Fair and Just World* on Social Media!

Share on Facebook

Share on Twitter

To purchase a print version of *God's Wisdom for a Fair and Just World* and for bulk discounts on the printed book, visit: https://www.truepotentialmedia.com/product/gods-wisdom-for-a-fair-and-just-world/
or use your smartphone camera on the flowcode image below to download a free copy or to purchase print a print copy of *God's Wisdom for a Fair and Just World*

Why I Wrote This Book

There is one lie powerful enough to seduce the entire world and compel all of humanity into anarchy, rebellion, rioting, and the destruction of civilization as we know it. It's playing out right now in the streets of major cities around the globe. Thankfully, it's not too late to discover the simple truth that can bring peace, safety, and justice to our world!

I have traveled to many countries throughout the world, talking to the citizens and many government officials. In most developing nations the corruption is unimaginable. The poor are desperately oppressed, while leaders are wealthy and corrupt. There is no such thing as equal justice.

What is happening in America and many of the first-world nations is not to make the nations better. It certainly is not to make our streets less violent or to create a better Constitution. What is happening in countries around the world is a game of deception. Through corrupt news media, with corrupt politicians' support, our citizens' ignorance is being exploited.

There are very real problems around the globe; however, every citizen living in a country where there is rioting, social unrest, and economic instability must realize that deceit is the tool. The exaggeration of real problems provides misdirection. While you're looking at the events unfolding before your eyes, those who intend to steal your freedom are robbing you blind! The goal is the collapse of your economy and the takeover of your country. Even this is a tool; it is not the goal. The goal is an elitist world, with no middle class, where there are the uber-wealthy and those who serve them.

Jesus foretold these events and provided the tools and strategies necessary to overcome these godless pursuits. In this book, I will remind you of Jesus' warnings and strategies. Then, like any sickness, a proper diagnosis can show us the path to the cure!

Believers need to stand for Jesus more than political figures, put godly values ahead of political correctness, and walk in love according to God's Word. More than being Woke, we are to be the light in a dark world, the salt that heals, and the standard that changes the world and restores true justice!"

THE OUTRAGE OF THE WORLD

The great outrage voiced in America and much of the world today is a cry for fair laws and equal application of those laws, i.e., Social Justice! A worldwide sense of inequality has inflamed this generation dramatically. It has spilled over into the streets, the halls of Congress, and even the aisles of churches, affecting every aspect of our daily lives.

Nearly every American believes there needs to be justice reform. But this ongoing pursuit of justice, as it is now, will end in less freedom for all citizens, whether black, white, Latino, Asian, Native American, or immigrant. The sad truth is that it will mean the loss of freedom for both minorities and the majority!

The predominant logic for establishing peace and fairness will end with elitist, globalists destroying life as we know it. It will usher us into a world that rejects all traditional societal norms, values, ethics, and morality! The wisest man to ever live gave this solemn warning, *"Do not associate with those given to change; For their calamity will rise suddenly, And who knows the ruin those two can bring?"* Proverbs 24: 21-22

The Hebrew word for *change* indicates *change driven passion.* It refers to following those who attempt to change societal norms, apart from God's wisdom for justice. The Scripture above connects with Paul's warning in Galatians against *heresies*, which refers to a party spirit, i.e., group-think, political parties, denominations, or merely following the passion of others. This kind of change is driven more by emotion and rage than logic and wisdom.

> The first step toward solving a problem is gaining a clear understanding of the problem.

The first step toward solving a problem is gaining a clear understanding of the problem. If we look at the facts, and the words of those inspiring the outrage, we discover there is no clear statement of the problem. The accusations have some merit, although the facts are vastly distorted. There is an abundance of emotional rhetoric about the situation. But emotions about a problem have little to do with the real problem.

Don't misunderstand, there are real problems that must be solved, but we are being deceived into focusing on and fighting the wrong battle. We are being led to answer the wrong questions. Presenting the wrong questions is a tactical distraction away from what is actually driving the conflict.

Emotional outrage about serious problems inspires rage about issues that have nothing to do with the real problem. Sadly, the body of Christ has replaced God's wisdom and Jesus' teaching with a corrupt logic that violates *the way of peace*. The moment we depart from God's wisdom, the way of peace, and love for one another, we fall into deception. We become co-conspirators with a philosophy that will destroy us all. The power of outside sources is not destroying us. We are killing ourselves because we believe the lies!

"So then, my beloved brethren, let every man be swift to hear, slow to speak, slow to wrath; for the wrath of man does not produce the righteousness of God." James 1: 19-20

When emotions drive us, we enter into what the Bible calls the works of the flesh. We give ourselves over to emotions like *hatred, contentions, jealousies, outbursts of wrath, selfish ambitions, dissensions, heresies, envy, and murders.* Then we convince ourselves that all this wickedness can somehow produce a godly outcome.

I wrote this book to help you realize what is happening in the world, how we got here, and the outcome if we continue this process. It will also help you understand the biblical wisdom for establishing a more just and fair world!

2

How Did We Get Here?

Few believers understand that the failure to interpret God's commandments in light of Social Justice always leads to a misunderstanding and misapplication of God's Word. Sadly, the way Jews and Christians have represented God, one might never consider that His Commandments and Social Justice are not just compatible, but essential to each other!

According to Dennis Prager, eight of the original ten Commandments were about relating to one another.[1] When Israel became a nation and needed to understand how to develop laws for social justice, God gave them a total of 613 commandments. These commandments were expansions on the original ten. This means that 490 of these commandments were about how we would walk in love one toward another. They were about civil order and social justice based on having value one for another.

One Hebrew scholar stated that the word translated *commandment* might best be rendered *prescription*. A prescription is something given to either prevent or heal sickness. God is love. He has called us to be like Him. He provided these prescriptions so we would know how to treat others in a manner that reflected His love and justice.

---

1   Dennis Prager, The Rational Bible: Exodus: God, Slavery and Freedom, Washington DC, Regnery Faith, 2018

Likewise, the word translated as *law,* in the Bible could be translated *signpost.* The law was a signpost. It was never a means to earn righteousness. As a signpost, it would reveal what our external behavior would look like if we walked in love from our hearts. Those who view laws and commandments as mere rules for outward observance misunderstand God's purpose for giving them. The founders of The US Constitution acknowledged that our Republic would only last as long as citizens embraced the morals and values presented in God's Word!

Without love (value) in their hearts for others, people have no internal motivation to obey the laws. Therefore, all civil laws must have penalties for those who violation them. The goal of penalties, however, was not to punish the offender. The goal was to provide benefits for everyone: the perpetrator, the victim, protection of the innocent, those too weak to protect themselves, the poor, and the observer.

Religion has perverted the understanding of what God has done in the past. Most Jews, Christians, and non-believers think the commandments were given for legalistic control or religious subservience. This belief reveals our ignorance of the Bible and history. A serious look at world history shows that God's commandments were the fairest code of civil justice ever given.

God's promise to Israel was that His code of civil justice would provide fair treatment for all citizens and immigrants, peace, and prosperity. He also said this would cause all nations to respect and fear them. In other words, this would provide peace and stability against all internal and external threats. The goal was to affect the entire world. Israel utterly failed on that goal, as did the church.

All nations self-destruct the same way. Corrupt politicians pass corrupt laws to advance their agendas, increase their wealth, and expand their power. Everything happening on the streets of America and other countries results from corrupt leaders rejecting God's wisdom for a fair and just world.

Are we so naïve as to think the leaders in Cuba, China, Venezuela, and other countries were unaware that their policies would thrust their citizens into financial desperation and poverty? Of course, they knew! It was part of their strategy to bring about a shift in wealth and power from the citizens to the elitists! Leaders making a grab for power and money always know the destruction their policies will bring. Yet, they have total disregard for those who will be negatively affected! This is the mindset of an elitist!

All nations that fail economically and socially, first fail morally and ethically. By rejecting God's morals, values, ethics, and standards, we reject God's wisdom. Observing God's standards as a basis for social justice is not about being a Christian or a Jew; it's about employing what has already been validated by historical evidence. None of these things are secrets. But they are hidden by the greedy and immoral!

The mob presents valid issues as their basis for demanding change. However, the changes they require have historically proven not to work. When any attempt for dialog is requested, they shift the focus and claim that their opponents do not want to solve the problem. People ignorant of history and the facts of the case are then easily manipulated, and ignorantly follow the mob.

The world is facing what the Bible calls iniquity or lawlessness. Its devastating outcome is not the judgment of a wrathful God; it is the fruit, i.e., the natural consequence, of gross foolishness!

12

The farther any nation moves away from God's social justice, the sooner it will collapse socially and economically. It will most certainly fail to maintain a fair system of social justice. The good news is that we can stop this flow of destruction, save millions of lives, and prevent the suffering of billions. But it has to start with believers who are willing to give up their religious ideologies and accept God's Word!

3

THE LIE WE ALL BELIEVE

Identifying counterfeit money begins by studying genuine money. The same is true when it comes to identifying a lie. It is impossible to recognize a lie until we know the truth!

A myth of monumental proportions is destroying the world. The church is the only body of people who have the resources to expose the lie, but the church has been beguiled! Just as Eve believed the serpent's lies in the Garden, the church believes the same lies. Eve and Adam thought they could have a better world by abandoning God and following their ideas of good, evil, and justice. This lie was the Luciferian inspiration that gave birth to humanism, which gave birth to socialism.

Socialism is the promise of a fair and just world. It is the hope of a utopian society by the eradication of all inequity. As it turns out, the Christian community is especially susceptible to this temptation. Socialism offers everything the Bible offers through entering the Kingdom of God. It is a call back to the original temptation: determine good and evil for yourselves and leave God out of it!

Modern Christians long to see the promise of God's Kingdom established on Earth. Unfortunately, they seem to ignore the fact that it is a work of the Holy Spirit (Romans 14:17) accomplished through the hearts of individual believers (Luke 17:21).

When someone has a passion for seeing a world as God promised it, combined with ignorance of Scripture, they are susceptible to what the Bible calls *iniquity*, or in some translations, *lawlessness*. Lawlessness does not merely reject society's laws; it rejects God's laws and commandments as the basis for justice.

Socialism promises the same quality of life God promises. The caveat is that in socialism, one must reject God and all His wisdom for justice. The philosophies of man must replace God's standards of morality, ethics, and justice. For the last 60-70 years, everything in American society has aimed at eradicating all knowledge of God. They continued to make God's promises, but they tried to fulfill them through the wisdom of men!

In the Garden of Eden, the serpent introduced a series of lies to the human race. Embracing those lies has been the basis for every pain and sorrow that has come into the world. Genesis 3:5 exposes the three most damning lies: *"For God knows that in the day you eat of it your eyes will be opened, and you will be like God, knowing good and evil."*

> Socialism fully embraces every lie presented in the Garden.

- By listening to God, you are blind.

- You are not really like God now; by disobeying Him, you will become like Him.

- The way to the ultimate life is to determine good and evil for yourself, apart from God's Word.

Socialism fully embraces every lie presented in the Garden. It rejects any notion of God as a destructive, limiting, religious myth. The path to ultimate fulfillment is the rejection of all morals and ethics presented in the Bible. The corrupt Luciferian logic says that you are not created in God's likeness and image; therefore, you have no control over your life or the events on Earth. Good and evil are subjective, based on current cultural trends and human laws.

In a perversion of compassion, the church has been complicit in a political movement that establishes all of humanity as gods, able to determine good and evil for ourselves! We have now reached a place where we call good evil and evil good The world was created on the foundation of righteousness. Its inhabitants were to flourish by remaining in harmony with the righteous Creator. When righteousness is perverted, all creation is out of harmony with God, and the foundations are destroyed, Psalm 11:3.

This book will open your eyes to God's wisdom for a fair and just world. This is not a call to give up your pursuit of justice; it is an opportunity to stay free from deception, restore peace, and establish justice.

However, socialism is not the real enemy. It is merely the tool, the means, i.e., the only deception powerful enough, to deceive the body of Christ and destroy the world. This book reveals the enemy: those who benefit most by seducing the world. It also explains the plan they have for you and other unsuspecting inhabitants of the globe. This false promise of justice will usher in more pain, suffering, and inequality than anything this world has ever witnessed! But it can only happen if we believe the lie!

4

IDENTIFYING THE REAL ENEMY

Once we identify the enemy, solving the problem is no longer a mystery! Knowing the enemy usually reveals the intent of its actions. However, when the enemy is an idea rather than a person, practical strategies to resolve the problem are complicated. Those who wish to destroy a country from within do not all fit neatly into a single category. There are usually multiple layers of motivations, starting with the very top: pure evil. However, not everyone participating in the destruction of a nation is working from a purely evil intention. Those who are motivated by greed and power are the culprits. All the chaos begins in their wicked motivations.

Many of the people on the street see a real cause that needs resolution. If a government were only dealing with this group, solving any social problem would be relatively simple. But the voices of those truly pursuing justice are rarely heard. The voices heard by the corrupt media are the agitators, the destroyers, those with money and power!

At least two groups of unreasonable people exist between the evil-doers and those seeking justice: the ideologues and the useful idiots. In modern society, these two groups have much in common. They are usually young, which means they have little life experience. They are taught the philosophies that drive their actions from an influential person, like a teacher, political influencer, manipulator, or religious leader.

These groups fall into a role of entitlement through one of two ways. Either they have lived an entitled life, with little personal responsibility, or they have suffered because of personal irresponsibility and consider themselves to be victims of an unjust society! The opposite of gratitude is entitlement. It doesn't matter how they arrived at their particular version of entitlement; the result is a justification of irrational thoughts and actions, giving rise to sociopathic tendencies. It doesn't matter who gets hurt as long as they get what they want!

According to Merriam-Webster.com/dictionary, the definition of Ideologue is - *"an often blindly partisan advocate or adherent of a particular ideology."*

Ideologues are generally extreme egotists. They very often consider themselves and their ideas superior to others. They become so self-invested in ideology, philosophy, or opinion they are willfully blind to facts that would prove them wrong. They have one goal: to prove themselves right no matter what the cost to others.

Useful idiots, like the ideologues, tend to be college graduates, who preferably have never had jobs. They have been influenced by propaganda from the college campus. Idealism that has never been proven to work fuels their passion. Quoteinvestigator.com says, *"Historically, the term 'useful idiot' has referred to a naive or unwitting ally of a ruthless political movement, especially a communist movement. Supposedly, Vladimir Lenin and Joseph Stalin used this expression contemptuously of non-communists who aligned themselves with their political positions."*

One common denominator of those who riot and seek to be in the spotlight is that they have seldom had jobs and never created businesses. When they have had jobs, they were often government jobs that required no personal risk. They have little understanding of how the real world works. Personal responsibility, sacrifice, and entrepreneurial thinking are foreign mindsets and often considered evil and unfair. Despite their ignorance, arrogance, and lack of a factual argument, they demand that everyone accept their logic as legitimate!

These people are irrational, ignorant idealists, believing the end justifies the means, regardless of the pain and suffering they cause. Their arguments are nothing more than propaganda handed down to them in talking points. The average citizen cannot see beyond the talking points, thereby becoming complicit in destroying civilization as we know it. But there is a way to get to the truth!

The strategies employed to reach a goal often reveal what is concealed! If we observe the wisdom of Jesus' teaching, we need only look to one Scripture to begin reverse engineering the problem from the cause. *"A tree is known by its fruit."* Matthew. 12:33

Suppose a person claims to pursue justice for himself while taking justice away from others. In that case, justice is not what he desires. Likewise, if someone says they want peace and tries to bring it about by chaos, peace is not the goal. So, what can we learn from this? Those who fight for change are not always in pursuit of the change they claim to seek! The means they use to accomplish change reveal what they seek!

Most people in the world have an excuse for being so easily duped. They have been brainwashed their entire lives by anti-God propaganda cloaked in Social Justice propaganda. The church, however, has no excuse. We have the very words of God. Jesus came, modeled, and explained how to interpret every Word of God. We reject God's morals, values, standards, and wisdom for justice because we do not believe God is as just, fair, and compassionate as those calling for us to reject God's justice. We are so deceived that we are ready to replace God's Word with something concocted by greedy, power-hungry, godless, religious and political leaders.

So, here are the questions we must answer, *"Can a mortal be more righteous than God? Can a man be more pure than his Maker?"* Job 4:17

Every time we say yes to a law, philosophy, or concept that seems fairer and more just than God's, we are saying, *"Yes, we are more righteous than God, our justice is fairer than God's."* According to Scripture, this lawlessness will usher us into global tribulation, rendering us so desperate the antichrist will deceive us!

Elitism is overthrowing the world. The goal is what the Bible presents as a One-World government that controls all the earth's resources. They are a small group of people who believe the planet's natural resources should be preserved for them and their progeny.

Elitists have contempt for the common man, but they also have contempt for God. History records that Solomon wrote a letter to the kings in the known world, warning them to rule justly. He talked about the fact that they did not know God and had no hope of eternal life; all they had was what they could amass in this life. When there is no abiding awareness of eternal life, the wicked have no moral boundaries!

Modern elitists do not believe that ordinary people have the right to consume the air they breathe because they are taking it away from those who deserve it. George Bernard Shaw, infamously stated that every person should have to come before a committee and justify why they should be allowed to live.

When speaking among their private groups, I have heard elitists, openly admit that hundreds of millions will die in the process of establishing this New World Order. They say they will try to kill them in the most merciful ways, but the price is justified regardless of how many die.

The justification for population control as a means to preserve the natural resources for a select group goes back as far as ancient Mesopotamia. It is encouraged by Fabian Socialists like George Bernard Shaw. National Socialists, Hitler, the Soviets, and the Communist Chinese implemented this ideology through their ruthless policies. In 1960s America, Bill Ayers and Bernardine Dohrn, domestic terrorist organization leaders of the Weather Underground, espoused and promoted this ideology. It was easy to find speeches online; however, in an attempt to hide their plan, many of these speeches have been taken down!

The Bible presents the facts that there is a real devil and there are wicked, greedy people. History has proven repeatedly that these people, like Lucifer, the one they follow, seek only to kill, steal, and destroy. Yet, the church and the world have made the fatal mistake. In the face of thousands of years of evidence, they refuse to admit that these people exist. Usually, they hesitate to protect the innocent, allowing thousands and sometimes millions to die before admitting the truth.

We would have prevented both World Wars if we had acted based on God's Word.

We would have prevented both World Wars if we had acted based on God's Word. Nearly two-hundred-million innocent people, through war and man-made famine, died in the communist overthrow of Europe and China. The same wickedness that brought about those horrific abominations is at work in our country and the world. Yet, we pretend nothing is going wrong!

Religious and political leaders close their eyes, pretending they do not see what is happening. We pretend not to see and not to know. Jesus warned that the world would ignore all the signs of the time and plunge into destruction, just as it did before Noah's flood! The problem is not that we do not see the signs of the time. The problem is, it is too inconvenient to do anything about what we see!

Why We Don't Want to Perceive

The Hebrew language of the Bible presents incredible insight into the concept of perception. Some are not willing to hear because they are unwilling to obey. Pride, arrogance, and personal opinions blind others. Finally, some don't perceive, because it would require them to change. They choose willful ignorance and pretend they don't know. Regardless of the subtleties, these three categories are all rooted in selfishness and pride.

The Hebrew words for *hear* and *obey* are a continuum. There is no difference between the two. The idea behind this word implies we are unable to hear, i.e., perceive from God, what we would not be willing to obey. Since hearing and perceiving occurs in the heart, we must realize that once we determine we want something, we harden our heart to anything that might prevent us from obtaining it!

Of course, some are so sure they are right that their ego will not let them realize any truth incongruent with what they have chosen. Jesus explained that insisting we see, makes us blind, John 9:41.

The last category is those who close their eyes, lest they should understand and change, Matthew 13:15. They don't want healing from their corruption and perversion.

The Lord is our Shepherd. He never stops attempting to lead.

However, He cannot lead where we are unwilling to go. But, we are all without excuse. Every human being on this earth realizes that hurting others is wrong. Every person who owned a slave knew it was wrong; every doctor or nurse who has aborted a baby knows it is wrong. Every murderer knows what he or she does is evil and wrong. However, like a blister that grows into a callous, if they continue in their evil long enough, their heart grows hard and insensitive, but God is still speaking!

> The religious leaders of Jesus' day, falsely implied that they would believe His teaching if only He would provide a sign.

The religious leaders of Jesus' day, falsely implied that they would believe His teaching if only He would provide a sign. This request was more than ironic, considering He had just miraculously fed thousands, with seven loaves of bread and a few fish. The significance of His response often goes unnoticed. *"You know how to discern the face of the sky, but you cannot discern the signs of the times."* Matthew, 15:32-16:4. They had already seen signs and wonders that proved the legitimacy of His claims. Moreover, Jesus performed the four Messianic miracles, which was the religious leaders' acid test by which they were to recognize the Messiah.

Why, after all the signs and wonders, would they continue to request further verification? Simple! They didn't want His message to be true! They didn't want the Messiah to disrupt their way of life and business! The religious leaders had a corrupt system providing them with wealth and power. Jesus' morals, values, and ethics would challenge the very systems by which they fulfilled the lust of their flesh!

Jerusalem's religious and political leaders may have suffered from the same normalcy bias syndrome that caused millions of Jews to lose their lives in Nazi Germany! The normalcy bias, or normality bias, is a cognitive bias that leads people to disbelieve or minimize the threat.[2]

There are several possible reasons intelligent people will ignore a massive threat:

- It is a problem is so overwhelming that to admit it would be more than one could bear.
- It is so far beyond the boundaries of our "normal," it cannot be cognitively perceived.
- It threatens to deprive us of the way we get what we want out of life.
- The overwhelming fear of the unknown

We are in a much more dire situation today than the religious leaders of Jerusalem. The Bible describes what we will soon face as the worst tribulation in the world's history, Mark, 13:19. Nearly every generation of Christians has believed theirs was the last. However, they were interpreting end-time prophesies based on regional events. We are the first generation to see specific prophecies fulfilled across the globe.

The reasons why any believer should be surprised by these global anomalies are all hollow excuses. Jesus warned these times would come. He explained how and why they would come. He told us how to know when they had begun. Jesus even explained the political ideology they would employ to overthrow the governments of the world. His Word also taught how we could prevent these times from coming! He made sure we would know the signs which would reveal this destructive season, so they would not take us unaware! Yet, we, like the Jews of Jerusalem and Nazi Germany, manufacture excuse after excuse to justify rejecting His Word and our responsibilities. We pretend to be ignorant of the magnitude of the problem.

---

2   https://en.wikipedia.org/wiki/Normalcy_bias

The body of Christ could have prevented all this devastation! The good news is, we can still act to diminish the carnage in our generation. We can create a just and fair world; this book explains how, in straightforward and easy to understand language! It all starts with reading the signs.

6

Can We Read and Understand the Signs?

These specific signs punctuate the times we face. Never before have Jesus' warnings occurred on a global scale. But we must remember, He warned us so we could either stop these events or know how to overcome them when the rest of the world is crumbling. This book is designed to satisfy either scenario.

Several of the following discussions and explanations are based on Matthew 24:4-15. Jesus' words are italicized for clarity. It is crucial to understand that when Jesus talks about *the end* in this passage, He is not talking about the end of time. I will explain as we consider His teachings.

Jesus began His teaching about the end with the dire warning to be aware of the deception. *"Take heed that no one deceives you!"* Jesus is exposing the fact that every tactic of destruction He will discuss is rooted in deception. If God's people do not succumb to deception, they can stop these events.

In 2 Corinthians 2:11, Paul points out that we can prevent Satan from taking advantage of us, by not being *"ignorant of his devices."* Almost every modern translation of the New Testament will translate *devices* as schemes, strategies, or plans.

The Greek word translated as *devices* means a mental perception or thought.[3] The critical factor in bringing worldwide destruction is a deception aimed at changing your perception. The first perceptional change is your view of God. When elitists launch their plan for a country, their major effort is toward demoralization. They cannot destroy a country that has a strong belief in God!

Their tactics include boosting immorality of all kinds. They put significant effort into normalizing and decriminalizing sex-crimes. Drug trafficking, human trafficking, prostitution, pornography, and pedophilia are normalized.

> Over time the most significant thing that must happen is silencing the voices of godly leaders and believers.

Normalizing these sinful deviant behaviors seduces people into rejecting God's morals and values. Over time the most significant thing that must happen is silencing the voices of godly leaders and believers. Once you've been deceived about God's goodness and relevance, the rest of the process is easy!

As this word implies, none of the tragedies described in these verses are what brings an end to the world as we know it! The way to destroy the world we know, the morals, values, ethics, and standards of justice, is rooted in spin and propaganda, i.e., the distortion of the facts! At this very moment, the global media is spinning world events to shape the perception of those listening to their twisted reports. People who believe false reporting are acting on perceptions, thereby playing into the hands of the destroyers!

Lies are weapons explicitly designed to alter your perception, which results in changing the way you think, plan, and make decisions. Deceit is the leaven to which the Bible refers. You are

---

3   Thayer's Greek Lexicon, Electronic Database. Copyright © 2000, 2003, 2006 by Biblesoft, Inc.

controlled by your opinions and ideologies by subtle internal thought, not by authoritative external sources.

In these pages, you will discover the truth behind the lies. You will be able to stabilize the fear attempting to take control of your decision-making process. You will have the one weapon that em-powers you to rise above the deception: truth!

7

WARS AND RUMORS OF WARS

Jesus is not describing things that define the arrival of the end of time! But He is describing events that lead to an end. These are signs of the times. We must, however, remember, He is not saying these are the end of times; He is saying these lead to an end, but it is not the end the church has understood it to mean. (I will clarify what the original language says.)

Providing this information equips the church to be the only entity on Earth capable of understanding what is happening, and what we can do to end this massive deception. Sadly, the church is not awake; much of the church does not trust Jesus as much as they trust the government and news media. Still, worst of all, much of the body of Christ is complicit in the very actions we have been equipped to stop!

The times Jesus describes are, without a doubt, a time of global wars and conflict. However, the keyword in this phase is *rumors* of wars. Thayer's Lexicon says that the Greek, for "rumor," could be translated as hearsay.[4] The element that drives people to surrender their freedom is not war, but the exaggerated rumors. Almost every war on the globe could be ended in a matter of months if we fought to win.

---

4   Thayer's Greek Lexicon, Electronic Database. Copyright © 2000, 2003, 2006 by Biblesoft, Inc. All rights reserved. # 189

Once again, He is warning of the subtle art of deception. There will be wars, but it is the rumors, exaggerations, bias, and slanderous reports that overcome men's hearts with fear! More than once, I have been in some remote part of the world doing mission work. My family would be fearful for my safety because of reports on CNN. When I was able to talk to them, I would calm their fears with the truth; the reports they heard were rumors and lies, not what was happening.

More than once, I have seen different video clips from one riot, cut into various scenes, then shown on the news to create the illusion of nationwide or city-wide rioting. The video was factual, but the facts were exaggerated for the purpose of altering perception!

Propaganda, according to the Oxford Dictionary, is information, especially of a biased or misleading nature, used to promote or publicize a particular political cause or point of view. **Almost nothing we see or hear on the news today is factual.** Almost nothing we see or hear on the news today is factual. What we see are snippets of speeches and events lifted out of context, as a way to change the meaning!

By lifting an event out of context, it is no longer true, even though the facts are presented. The Hebrew word for truth is very enlightening. It tells us that we must know what happened before an event and its outcome before we can ascertain the event's validity. We think what we see at this moment is the truth.

Gossip, slandering, or repeated tales have the goal of separating friends, i.e., turning people against one another. Every day, biased news media outlets worldwide do not report the news; they tell their version of events. Credible news media coverage is almost non-existent! News companies function primarily as the propaganda arm of those seeking to recreate our world.

Christians have become lazy. It is easier and more comfortable to violate God's Word than to be responsible for what we hear and believe. Proverbs 18:17 says, *"The first to present his case seems right, till another comes forward and questions him."* (NIV) No matter how convincing the story about any event may be, we are warned against reaching an opinion until we have heard the other side of the story. The propagandist never allows you to listen to the other side of the story!

Due process is a factor that defines the US legal system. Due process is straight out of God's code of civil justice. Due process says a person is innocent until proven guilty. Both sides must be heard, and witnesses must corroborate their statements. With mob rule, there is no regard for God's Word nor the rule of law. Daily, we see people tried in the court of public opinion with no respect for God's code of justice. We assume those who scream the loudest, feigning outrage, are telling the truth. Or even worse, we pretend, since they are the party we support, that they are always truthful! This is willful self-deception!

> We fail to realize that when the rule of law has been totally destroyed, it will be us on trial for our faith, and there will be no one left to fight for our rights!

Sadly, gossip, slander, and tale-bearing have become commonplace in the church. We don't protest. We don't stand for those eviscerated by the press; there is no outrage. We passively sit and hold our peace. We fail to realize that when the rule of law has been totally destroyed, it will be us on trial for our faith, and there will be no one left to fight for our rights! Whether we hear it on the news or from a friend, we have a moral obligation to know if something is true by God's standards, before we believe it, agree with it, support it, or act on it!

8

Do Not Become Troubled

"See that you are not troubled; for all these things must come to pass, but the end is not yet."

It is almost unbelievable that Jesus would tell us not to become troubled in light of all these horrific events. Let's consider the wisdom of His words. First and foremost, the most destructive emotion in the Bible is fear. Fear exists in the continuum of unbelief. Fear is both a cause of disbelief as well as the result of unbelief! Fear is the thief that never stops stealing!

Fear makes it completely impossible to hear God's voice in our hearts. Fear put's us into fight or flight mode. It renders us incapable of maintaining any mindset that promotes love and kindness. It propels us into sheer survival mode, regardless of who gets hurt or how irrational our logic.

But there is another factor I want to focus on: none of these events indicate that we have crossed the line to the *end!* In the original language, the word *end* can mean: to set out for a definite point or goal; properly, the point aimed at as a limit, i.e. (by implication) the conclusion of an act or state.[5]

---

5   Biblesoft's New Exhaustive Strong's Numbers and Concordance with Expanded Greek-Hebrew Dictionary. Copyright © 1994, 2003, 2006 Biblesoft, Inc. and International Bible Translators, Inc. NT:5056

From this definition, we see that all the events occurring during this time have a goal. They are not random! Allowing the spread of unchecked lawlessness has the purpose of bringing an end to something, to open the way to something else. That which is coming to an end is a just, fair, civil society; that which emerges will be a society of lawlessness.

Lawlessness, as used in Scripture, is not just the breaking of man's laws. It is rejecting and violating God's laws as the basis for love and social justice and replacing them with man's laws.

> The good news is that, at this stage, we have not yet passed the point of no return.

The good news is that, at this stage, we have not yet passed the point of no return. Jesus said all these events were the beginning of sorrows. The word *sorrows* is used to describe a woman having birth pangs. In other words, these things are being inflicted on the world by the wicked for the specific purpose of giving birth to a New World Order, i.e., a world with no knowledge of God! This New World Order will be a new system of government which will end freedom as we know it. It will unleash unfathomable immorality and inhuman treatment against the poor by the elite. All people will either be in the ruling class or property of the State!

Fear is paralyzing. It keeps us from proactively or reactively responding. It can emotionally drown us by the sheer magnitude of circumstance. After all, the goal of the massive deceptions is to make us fear we can do nothing about the situation. Possibly the most destructive is the fear of taking a stand; the fear of letting our voices be heard while we can make a difference!

As anti-God lawlessness and rebellion intensify, it becomes more and more apparent that all those people screaming for justice have no interest in justice as we understand it. They want to take away the rights of all who dare to disagree with their concept of justice.

They silence all who express a difference of opinion. Businesses are boycotted and destroyed for merely disagreeing with some extreme political views, or for liking an opinion they reject. Elitism not only tells you what you can do, it tells you how you should think!

A church in Birmingham, Alabama that helped thousands of poor and needy people throughout the area faced the wrath of a politically motivated city because the pastor "liked" comments that were different from those in power. Since I first wrote these pages, several churches have disappeared from social media. Their voices have been silenced.

People are afraid to state their opinions, put a flag on their house, a political bumper sticker on their car, or even honestly answer a polling question for fear of reprisals. It's time we all realize that these groups have no interest in helping anyone other than themselves. If we remain silent, we will soon be like the people of China, faced with losing all state benefits unless they denounce Jesus as Lord, destroy all religious paraphernalia, and pledge their allegiance to the chairman of the communist party as Lord!

Here are the options presently offered:

- Enjoy momentary freedom from persecution now by keeping silent.

- Continually surrender your freedoms in exchange for the illusion of independence.

- Deny Jesus as Lord, and serve the elite.

- Stand for God and real justice!

In countries that have been overthrown by socialism and communism, much of the church did nothing. They convinced themselves that remaining silent might allow them to help the needy for a while. They preached what they were allowed to preach and, little by little, become a cog in the propaganda machine! By the time they realized their mistake, it was too late!

9

NATION WILL RISE AGAINST NATION

In Matthew 24:7, Jesus warned of wars and rumors of wars. Then He described two different types of conflicts: nation against nation and kingdom against kingdom. Kingdom against kingdom is more like war as we understood it in the 20th century, i.e., one country fighting another country. However, warfare has changed dramatically over the past century.

Recent wars have proven that a superpower cannot be overthrown by a nation-to-nation confrontation. The best way to defeat a superior power is from within. Since Vietnam, America has lost militarily for a few simple reasons. The Vietnamese knew the American media would win the war for them. They were more than willing to sacrifice thousands of their own to accomplish their objective. They knew the American news media would shame Americans into eventually pulling out of the war.

The second factor was our government would not let us win the war, even though it was within our means to do so. Ridiculous rules of engagement and illogical limitations on where we could attack did nothing but prolong the war. But why win a war, when it was making billions of dollars for your constituents, who would then use their money and influence to keep you in office? We lost Vietnam internally to greed and propaganda!

The Ming dynasty ruled in China for centuries. They were the most secure nation in the world. The Forbidden City (which I have visited) was an impenetrable fortress. It was the most protected national capital in the world. It protected their emperor, his family, and the royal court. The Great Wall, which was over five-thousand miles long, was their defense from the barbarian hordes to the north. As a nation, they were impregnable! Invasion into the country and especially the capital, was unfathomable.

Their collapse was not, however, the result of a superior foreign power. The destruction of the Ming Dynasty came about because of a corrupt military leader who took bribes from the enemy in exchange for passage through the Great Wall.

America has its faults, as do all endeavors that rely on the integrity of people! Until people are perfect, no government will be perfect. I have traveled to many countries throughout the world, talking to citizens and government officials. In most developing nations the corruption is unimaginable. The poor are desperately oppressed! In many countries, leaders are wealthy and corrupt. There is no such thing as equal justice.

> Through corrupt news media, with the support of corrupt politicians, the ignorance of our citizens is being exploited.

The corruption happening in America and many first-world nations is not aimed at making a better nation; it certainly is not to make our streets less violent or to create a better Constitution. What is happening in countries around the world is a global game of deception. Through corrupt news media, with the support of corrupt politicians, the ignorance of our citizens is being exploited. This has gone on in third world countries for centuries, but the deception happening in first-world nations today is broadcast worldwide by corrupt news organizations.

A few small domestic terrorist factions, a complicit media, and corrupt politicians are being used by global elitists working a far more vile agenda. Massive global violence is not designed to destroy a country completely. What is occurring in numerous countries is intended to weaken the government, destabilize the nations by destroying unity, and collapse their economy to create such desperation and suffering that all the nations of the world will surrender to the globalist elitists in order to be to saved. All it takes to accomplish this is greedy, power-hungry ideologues who intend to eliminate all knowledge of God from the world.

Every citizen living in a country where there is rioting, social unrest, and economic instability must remember that deceit is the tool, socialism is the way, but neither of these is the goal. These are only the delivery systems! The goal is a godless world, controlled by a handful of anti-god elitists!

Jesus told us of the tools and strategies that would be used to accomplish these godless pursuits. Since we know the disease, we know the cure! Today, if believers will actually stand for Jesus more than political figures, put godly values ahead of political correctness, walk in love according to God's Word more than Wokeness, we will be the standard that changes the world and restores true justice!

10

CULTIVATING ETHNIC WARFARE

In Matthew 24:7, Jesus reveals an integral aspect of the disinformation campaign used to create war, riots, and social conflict on a global scale. The KJV says, *"Nation will rise against nation."* In the original language, it says, *ethnos* shall rise against *ethnos*. This word is referring to ethnic groups!

When we first think of ethnic groups, we tend to think only of racial distinctions. However, according to the Oxford Dictionary, ethnicity is the result of breaking down the population into many different kinds of groups: national, cultural, traditional, tribal, ancestral, racial, and more.

He is describing, within the context of His opening warning, splintering countries into as many factions as possible. Deceit, i.e., propaganda, will then be used to magnify strife, fighting, jealousy, and hatred between the factions.

This would be a good time for believers to remind themselves that hatred, contentions, jealousies, outbursts of wrath, selfish ambitions, dissensions, heresies (groupthink), envy, murders, drunkenness, revelries, and the like, are works of the flesh, Galatians 5:20-21. Any Christian supporting or agreeing with this approach as a means to solve problems is in direct opposition to God, regardless of the motive or the need!

God endeavors for men to solve problems through mutual respect, unity of purpose, open honest dialog, and biblical justice! This is called *the way of peace*. The wicked do not pursue *the way of peace;* follow the way of chaos and destruction. The Bible speaks of those using carnal, cruel tactics when it says, *"the way of peace they have not known."* Romans 3:17 It is never godly to create division or to employ any of the works of the flesh to accomplish a desired outcome. When agitators stir mobs to violence, God's Justice, and the law of the land, should be immediately used to stop them.

Karl Marx, an avowed Communist, and Satanist realized he could only seduce the world into communism with the untenable promises of socialism. In fact, it is believed that Marx saw socialism as the only lie powerful enough to destroy the entire world! So, what do socialism, communism, and satanism have to do with what is happening in the world today?

Globalist elitists create overwhelming fear by using propaganda to blow conflicts entirely out of proportion. They create a strawman to blame for the problem and then offer a solution that requires surrendering personal freedom.

There are genuine problems in America and other countries. Still, one thing you can be sure of: those controlling the media, and offering solutions that violate God's justice, are the ones who created and inflated the problems. The world they seek to create will only be a utopia for them; it will be hell on earth for the rest of us.

In the 1930s, a black man, Manning Johnson, became a communist. He believed they were sincerely trying to improve conditions for his people. But like many blacks who became communists, it didn't take long to realize the wicked and corrupt agenda of communism. As he put it, *"They had no interest in helping the black community, they intended to use his people as cannon fodder in a bloody revolution to destroy America."*

As early as 1928, the communists recognized that racial issues in America would be their means of destroying our nation. Manning Johnson authored *Color, Communism and Common Sense*. Anyone who wants to understand the real reason for the ethnic wars plaguing the world should read his book.

Ethnic wars in first-world countries are caused by a little bit of truth mixed with a massive amount of propaganda, void of facts, and inflamed by professional agitators who create the illusion of a monumental problem.

You might ask, what does communism have to do with America? Communism is no longer a threat; the Cold War is over! After World War II, the Soviet Union became synonymous with communism, which was viewed, by Americans, as a political party. However, communism and socialism are not just political; they have religious roots in satanism! They are working a religious agenda to eliminate the knowledge of God from the earth! Their murderous divisiveness is not the end; it is the means to the end!

Ethnic wars in first-world countries are caused by a little bit of truth mixed with a massive amount of propaganda, void of facts, and inflamed by professional agitators who create the illusion of a monumental problem. Socialism is the seductive solution to an instigated problem. In America, racism is the weak place in the wall that has been bombarded by the enemy for at least a hundred years.

We must remind ourselves before moving forward that communism is not a country or even a political movement. Communism is an ideal that promises a utopian society by rejecting God's morals, values, and ethics. Its promise is a paradise where you can fulfill all the lusts of your flesh with no guilt.

One of the incredibly effective propaganda tactics is to present socialism as if it is not communism. But, as Marx and others have pointed out, socialism is a transitional step into communism. Many agitators inflaming violence in the streets would not sacrifice their lives to such a wicked cause if they realized the outcome. For many, it took decades of brainwashing in grammar-school, high school, colleges, and universities to bring them to their current misdirected zeal.

They agitate and riot to usher in socialism, which they only know as a theory. They have no understanding of how it will affect them. A few years ago, I saw an enlightening undercover report. They asked students if they were in favor of socialism and the students expounded on the goodness of socialism. Then they were asked to share their computers with other students. The moment they were asked to make any sacrifice, they emphatically refused.

College students, those struggling to make a living, and yes, many Christians have been duped into believing in the strawman. They do not see the wealthy as job creators; they do not realize the benevolence of the wealthy; they have created an imaginary image of a wicked people hoarding money as children starve on the streets in front of the lavish homes of the wealthy. They never realize that they may soon be labeled as the wealthy and then their belongings will be appropriated.

Socialism is first accepted in the form of delusional idealism that must be fought for at any cost! Those who turn away from God's Word and surrender to the propaganda cooperate and sacrifice more and more to create the utopia that never comes. By the time they awaken from their delusion, it is too late!

Since socialism never works, they must create more strawmen, i.e., people to blame for its failure. Those who hold to any moral or ethical concepts are blamed as the reason socialism isn't working. These people must be eliminated. Continual brainwashing conditions the population to surrender one freedom at a time until they are forced into communism. They are conditioned to accept the philosophies of socialism. After all, they now realize that those who do not comply are eradicated. The more governmental powers are consolidated, the more inequality, poverty, and abuse of power expand!

Like all cults, the leaders never accept responsibility for their failed promises.

Like all cults, the leaders never accept responsibility for their failed promises. The people's *"lack of commitment"* is always the culprit! *"You just need to be more dedicated! You need to sacrifice more."*... blah, blah, blah! You need to convince yourself more deeply that the lie is true. Every failed promise, for which leaders refuse to accept responsibility, leads to a demand for more sacrifice from the followers. This continual increase in commitment will always come down to rejecting Jesus as Lord and swearing ultimate allegiance to the State!

What few will ever know is this: just as socialism is a transition into communism, communism is a transition to satanism. Most of Karl Marx's books have never been read outside of Russia. The Communists do not want the world to know how satanism drove the creation of communism.

Karl Marx was a pure Satanist. He was not like people who think satanism is about sex, drugs, and sin. Unlike many Satanists, he has no illusion of the remotest possibility of Satan defeating God. Unlike many Christians, a true Satanists knows the battle between God and the devil is determined. It was won the moment Jesus rose from the dead. Marx wrote that he knew he would spend eternity in hell; his only joy would be the millions of people he would take with him. True Satanists know all they can do to hurt God is to hurt what He loves most: humankind! They are fully committed to compelling people by deception or torture to reject God. Do most socialists know this? No! But this is the real goal.

CREATING A WORLD OF VICTIMS

A healthy society will never believe the lie of socialism. It takes decades of disruption, propaganda, and brainwashing to consider that socialism has any validity. Moving the citizenry from God based morals and values requires brainwashing into a very particular mindset; a victim mentality.

Remember, socialism promises a fair and just world where all things are shared equally. There must be the widespread belief that rampant inequality exists before one can consider a need for socialism. It takes decades and the diligent efforts of many tireless participants to make this corrupt goal into a reality!

It would seem to require a massive number of conspirators to transform an entire world, but all it takes is a handful of the wealthiest, anti-God elitists on the globe. Their followers do not need to understand their real intentions; they need only to be greedy or idealistic.

Corrupt, wealthy people spend billions of dollars on elections for the simple goal of provisioning a high budget campaign for a candidate that embraces anti-God principles. The wealthiest people in the world are the financiers of the elitist agenda. They want people with influence. Politicians have legislative powers, people in media have a voice and a platform; those in entertainment influence demoralization, union leaders can significantly affect the economy.

Educators are the category that may be more influential than any other for the long-game. Educators shape the world paradigm of millions of children. Much of what is playing out in the streets of America is the fruit of educators! These young, angry, violent, rebellious people did not spend their lives getting an education. They did sit in classrooms from the first grade through graduate school, but what they got was not education; it was brainwashing.

Throughout most of modern history, the US was number one among industrialized countries in education. Today, according to the Organization for Economic Cooperation and Development (OECD) 2018-2019 report, the US is number 25 in math, science, and reading. In some large cities, no child is functioning at their grade level in reading or math. When these students graduate with a diploma they did not earn, they will not be capable of competing in the job market.

Reading is the one skill the Bible commands us to have. People who can't read can't do research; they only know what others tell them. The thing stolen from all people who can't read is the Word of God. What could be better for those who desire to destroy a nation than hordes of angry, misinformed, radicalized young people? Actually, there is one better thing: angry, misinformed, radicalized, inexperienced, ignorant people, incapable of discovering the truth for themselves.

In America, there are four primary points emphasized in the educational system:

- America is evil.
- Socialism is good.

- God is a myth.
- Every white person is a privileged, bigoted, racist.

These young people have been overwhelmed by an imaginary problem that must be destroyed. They feel morally obligated to destroy the world as it is. They illogically destroy all societal norms in the name of justice, while violating every standard of morality and common sense!

They are angry at the world; they project the hatred on one another and themselves. Whether minority, poor, or wealthy, they all emerge with a victim's mentality! Regardless of class or color, they all blame someone for any part of their life that is challenging. If you're poor, it's someone else's fault. If you're rich, you should be ashamed. If you're white, you are privileged. You are racist, whether you know it or not! If you're a minority, everything that has gone wrong was deliberately perpetrated because of racism.

The logical penance for being white is to hate America, embrace self-hatred, and commit to the demise of this corrupt system. After a decade or two of being taught that America is filled with inequality, students become deeply convinced that a more equitable system of government must be developed. The same people who created the delusional judgment offer a solution that will not work, has never worked, and never will work. But these young, passionate radicals are too ignorant and biased to do personal research! They learned a false version of history. They ignorantly believe that socialism has worked all around the world. Based on the lie they have accepted, it is easy to understand their irrational, destructive behavior!

Remember, Jesus said the great deception of our times would lead to wars based on ethnicity. Those elitists who use socialism and communism as their platform for subversion identified nearly one hundred years ago that racism was America's Achilles heel! As it turns out, ethnic conflict has been the prescribed way they would divide and destroy America and many nations of the world!

Victims are hurting, but those with a victim's mentality are angry and seeking revenge. Christians can only claim victimhood by denying that God's Word will light the path, and His Spirit will strengthen them as they make the journey into the promises of God. We don't need to give our pity; we need to give hope and help that says, "Stand up and walk with God!" To support a victim's mentality is to reject the grace of God!

RACISM

Jesus also said, *"nation shall rise against nation,"* Matthew 24:7. The Greek word "nation" is actually ethnos," i.e., races. Racial (ethnic) conflict has always been a key strategy for destroying nations!

According to The Oxford Dictionary, racism is prejudice, discrimination, or antagonism directed against a person or people based on their racial or ethnic group, typically one that is a minority or marginalized.

Today racism has been redefined. According to the new Woke rules, it seems only white people can be racists. Given the new definition of racism, it turns out, the cry for racial justice appears to be more of a battle cry for revenge and punishment! All of this is complicated by radicals who mix themselves into groups that otherwise may be seeking peaceful solutions. The troublemakers change the narrative.

Today's radicals ignore the fact that Dr. Martin Luther King made more significant advances towards equality than had ever been made in our country. Dr. King didn't promote revenge and vengeance; he promoted equality. He didn't ask for special treatment of blacks; he asked for equal opportunity. He was adamantly committed to peaceful protests.

When Dr. King was assassinated, the wannabes that surrounded him turned his efforts into an opportunity for personal gain more than equal opportunity. Chaos and rioting launched an opportunity for personal profiting. Instead of making peace, they used chaos. Marxists revolutionism replaced biblical peace.

As believers, we must ask, "Who changed the rules and definitions of racism?" The new enlightenment is certainly not based on God's Word. Yet much of the church so casually tosses God's Word away without a thought of the consequences. Pastors encourage riot and revolution! A non-sensical, illogical, irrational series of demands have replaced meaningful communication. Now that only whites can be racists, there is no process that demands responsibility of all races. In fact, redefining racism delegitimizes issues that need addressing. It is an irrational presentation of the problem, which breeds irrational responses.

Racism is racism, no matter which race expresses it, to whom, or about whom, they express it. According to God's Word, we are to love one another, regardless of race or economic status. Those who do not walk in love are not only destroying themselves; they are destroying the one they swear to protect. Yet, political and even religious leaders justify the self-destructive behavior of minorities as an act of compassion. I was appalled when a politician was asked, *"What do you have to say about the burning of buildings, robberies, and violence taking place in the streets?"* This person who uses their religion when it benefits them, responded, *"People will do what people do."*

Leaders who justify bad behavior are like enabling parents who, for their own emotional benefit, will not teach, correct, or allow their children to face the consequences of bad behavior. When children are given constant excuses for bad behavior, they tend to become adults who violate rules, boundaries, and laws, expecting exemption from consequences.

Bob Woodson, a black man who was active in the civil rights movement of the 1960s, has strong condemnation for black leaders and politicians who create problems for personal benefit. He points out that they only have a job and make money as long as there is racial conflict!

Between manipulative politicians, corrupt preachers, revisionist teachers, and activist judges, it is a challenge for any child to become an emotionally healthy adult. Those made to feel like they are victims rarely develop one of the most important biblically-based attitudes for a healthy life: gratitude! Gratitude doesn't focus on what's wrong, and it doesn't deny what is wrong; it looks for what is right! Gratitude is thankful for what it does have, not angry about what it doesn't have.

The opposite of gratitude is entitlement. The entitled feel others owe them. In their minds, it is the world's responsibility to make them happy, healthy, and prosperous. If they are not successful and happy, they are being victimized.

One of the great lies of socialism is that all people deserve an equal outcome. Many Christians ignorantly think this position represents God's sense of equality. The Bible and the Constitution do not promote equal outcome, but equal opportunity. One of God's earliest commands to humans *be fruitful and multiply.*

God gave man freedom of choice. The earth provided natural resources. It was man's choice to go where they wanted to go and find the place and opportunity where they believed they could prosper! The Spirit of God is the Helper, not the doer. He works in the lives of those who choose to *do*. God requires all men, regardless of race, education, or background to, realize that He can empower us all to succeed when we trust and apply His wisdom for success.

Socialism says there should be no winners or losers; everyone should be a winner. Through education and assistance programs, both minorities and whites compete in programs where everyone is declared a winner. Nursery books that have been used for centuries to teach young people to work and be responsible have been rewritten to expound socialistic virtues. Personal responsibility is construed as white privilege and replaced by the anti-God message that children of all colors are entitled to the life they desire. Based on the definition of entitled, even when they get what they believe they are entitled, they will never be grateful. Therefore, they will always feel lack!

Children who are fed this constant diet of equality by suppressing success cannot compete in the real world. Dealing with failure is one of the most important lessons that should be learned by children. Having a sense of self-worth that is not based on success is the key to healthy relationships that are not ego-driven.

This is where the church should step up and teach people to make God their source. Believers should learn about the power of living in their new identity! The church must step up to the one overarching commandment given by Jesus: "*make disciples of all nations*" (ethnos). Instead, we have rejected God's Word for something that benefits us, isn't much trouble, and fulfills our carnal sense of success.

Developing disciples takes years. More than anything, however, it takes individuals who are making the journey for themselves. A disciple accepts the Master's teaching and makes it the foundation for life. Making disciples leads the new convert on the path of life, but it also keeps the seasoned believer on the firm foundation of truth! Everyone benefits!

> I can't speak for the rest of the world, but the real racism destroying America is political racism.

Few churches make disciples. Instead, they make converts. In many cases, they don't even make converts to Jesus; they make converts to their denomination. This is why we have billions of people worldwide who call themselves Christian but know nothing about God. In many cases, they follow a misguided compassion and oppose God!

Jesus didn't say to teach certain ethnic groups to be disciples; He said all ethnicities. Our unspoken message to minorities has been, "You are so oppressed, God can't help you!"

I can't speak for the rest of the world, but the real racism destroying America is political racism. There will always be challenges when people of different cultures attempt to live together. That's not a racial problem; it is cultural. The real racism, however, is the political leaders and profiteers who create division and hatred between the races for personal gain. If there is anything history has taught us, it is that when those who benefit from conflict suddenly appear in a situation they can exploit, there is never peace!

The Great Shaking

In Matthew 24:7, Jesus continues, *"And there will be famines, pestilences, and earthquakes in various places."* The word pestilences is not in the Bible's original language, although it would not be assumed it would occur. Famines and earthquakes are, however, in the original text!

It is extremely important to understand that God causes none of the things Jesus described in these Scriptures. These are not acts of God; they are acts of man! In the communist takeover of Europe and China, famine was an economical means of eliminating millions of people!

Famine provides plausible deniability for those who created the problem. The masses are convinced these are acts of nature. Religious people say it is an act of God. In the end, God gets blamed for that which evil people do!

Famine can be translated *scarcity of food or hunger.* It does not explicitly mean a lack of food because of natural factors like flooding or drought! More people have died of starvation, in modern times, because of deliberately engineered famine.

Venezuela was a prosperous nation just a few years ago. They were seduced by the lies of socialism. In 2017 people in Venezuela lost an average of a little more than 24 pounds per person. Once again, the promise of socialism manifested itself in elitism, diverting all the available resources to the elite!

Earthquakes are on the rise around the globe. Even earthquakes are the result of man's destruction of the earth. Wherever dams are built, there is an increase in earthquakes. The weight of the water in man-made lakes cannot be supported by the earth. Likewise, It is insane to think we can extract millions of gallons of oil out of the earth and not have geological shifts. Underground nuclear testing no doubt contributes to these problems.

Interestingly, the Greek word *earthquake* can mean *a shaking* of any kind. All of the world crises mentioned above will certainly cause a shaking. That's what they are designed to do. The elitists want to shake your hope and faith in God. They want you to feel so desperate and helpless that you will sell your soul for food or protection.

The strategy of the elitists is to create such fear, hardship, and desperation that you will have to turn to the government to save you.

The Bible speaks of a time that many theologians call the great falling away. People will abandon their faith and turn away from God! Religion has convinced most of the church world that these horrific events are the wrath of God. The church that was supposed to establish our faith will be a tool that undermines faith. Who will trust God if they believe God is causing the horrors that kill innocent children? The strategy of the elitists is to create such fear, hardship, and desperation that you will have to turn to the government to save you.

When you are alienated from God in your heart, they have accomplished their ultimate goal. Their goal is not to simply control you. The ultimate goal to use you as a pawn; the only pain they can bring to God is to destroy the human race for which Jesus died!

PANDEMICS, HEALTHCARE, AND TOTAL CONTROL

World leaders have long embraced the idea that without wars, it would be impossible to stabilize a country, stimulate the economy, and provide population control. This poses a unique problem for globalists!

There was a UN think group many years ago looking for ways to stabilize the world when there is only one government. One concept supporting the need for war is this: a common enemy will bond us together as a country. They concluded, in the absence of the fear of attack by another country, they could stimulate other fears. They must, however, create overwhelming life-threatening fear to such a degree people would believe only the government could help! Their suggestions were as bizarre as making people believe there was an alien invasion and as simple as creating pandemics.

People are desperately afraid of sickness. They have no awareness that allopathic medicine often interferes with the body's natural healing process. In many cases, the treatment can cause side-effects far more dangerous than the sickness! According to many healthcare professionals, almost all modern drugs interfere with the mitochondria, reducing energy, hampering immune function, causing chronic fatigue, and other chronic illnesses.

Americans' fear of sickness is punctuated by the fact that almost every study says Americans spend more money on health care per capita than any nation in the world, yet we tend to rank dead-last in quality of life. What this means is that we will keep spending the money on something that doesn't work because we're afraid. We believe we must have it! (On a positive note, western medicine is incredible at emergency medicine).

People naively think nationalized healthcare would make everyone's health care equal, and it would! It would all be equally bad!

For the elitists, nationalized healthcare is the death grip on a free society! People naively think nationalized healthcare would make everyone's health care equal, and it would! It would all be equally bad! Ask any veteran about the reliability of government healthcare. These men and women go to the hospital with a minor infection and die waiting for treatment. Do you love the service at the DMV? This question usually sends people into a tirade. Everyone knows that anything the government gets involved in becomes more expensive, less efficient, and loses every aspect of human compassion!

Besides the fact that the quality of health care will plummet, these agencies will, at some point, base eligibility for health care on the cost, age of the patient, and what they are deemed to contribute to society!

The rabbit hole doesn't end there. With government healthcare, they can force you to take treatments you do not want to take. You will lose all freedom of choice. Once the government controls our health care, we can all be eliminated at the whim of the government, by simply requiring a specific group of people to take a vaccine.

One of the most alarming things that will happen immediately is forced vaccinations. There is mounting evidence that vaccinations are dangerous. But it is already becoming obvious that they provide a means of government control. In other countries, vaccinations are mandatory. People are told that if they do not take the upcoming coronavirus vaccination, they will not have access to their retirement benefits, they will not be allowed to travel, they will not be allowed to interact with society, and other limitations.

You might ask, *"Are you against vaccinations?"* I'm against anyone losing their freedom of choice, and I am against anyone putting anything in my body without knowing what it is and its side-effects."

The elitists in America are drooling with anticipation. This will finally give them what the Bible warned would come: a way of marking and tracking people globally. They will insist that it is to protect us from exposure to those who might give us a disease. It will also be presented as a compassionate way of protecting others. What they really mean to say is, *"This will be our way of taking every freedom you now have!"* Even though the Bible warns of this, Christians keep convincing themselves that it will never come to that.

By definition, a coronavirus is a form of pestilence. In our modern world, epidemics will most likely be created in a lab for biological warfare. Then they will be unleashed on the earth to reduce the population, destabilize the existing economy, create massive fear and chaos, and take control of the "new" economy. Who would have believed that a virus that is not proven to be any more deadly than a seasonal virus could destabilize the global economy, close churches, and violate so many of our fundamental human rights?

Chaos produces uncertainty and fear. Fear and uncertainty push people into exchanging freedoms for security. But the whole thing is like a Ponzi-scheme. The rich and powerful create a problem, and the media exaggerates the situation to escalate fear and hysteria. Then the rich get richer by selling a cure for the problem. At this point, those who don't know God intimately have no source of security other than the government.

In America, governors and mayors are stepping beyond their legal authority, violating Constitutional rights, and refusing to consider any version of the facts that would limit their power!

Look how unleashing the coronavirus on the world has panicked citizens into giving up their rights. We do not receive consistent, accurate information about how the virus started. From the very beginning, medical advice has been contradictory and highly biased. In America, governors and mayors are stepping beyond their legal authority, violating Constitutional rights, and refusing to consider any version of the facts that would limit their power! There is ample evidence that the professionals, telling what treatment to avoid and what treatment to use, will massively profit from the treatment prescribed by the government!

Based on symptoms alone, hospitals, schools, and industries send people home and report them as positive for the coronavirus. We were told, at one point, the tests were only 50% accurate. Patients with a cold, the flu, or other viruses are reported as positive, even when they are not tested. There have been people who died from gunshot wounds and automobile accidents reported as coronavirus deaths. It is commonly reported that doctors must skew the numbers to make it look as if the virus is spreading. The media uses this misinformation to frighten you into submission. But you are not allowed to work, go outside, be with your family or go to church.

The coronavirus, which is real, has been used as a propaganda generator that could potentially destroy the US economy. If the

US economy collapses, it could have a global domino effect. Just think, if this much damage and chaos occur with a virus less deadly than annual influenza, imagine what can happen with famine, a real epidemic, or economic collapse.

Just consider this: the Bible teaches that washing with water and going outside in the sunlight is the best curative action to stop the spread of disease. Even medical science supports that. But we were told we had to stay indoors. Statistics reveal, when people stay indoors, the spread of the virus escalated. Everything we've been told is entirely or partially incorrect. Yet, we followed the advice of elitists who stand to profit, without questioning the efficacy of their guidance. Even if you didn't know the medical facts, just knowing what the Bible says should be enough to make a believer stop and think! Yet, the church readily casts aside the infallibility of the Creator for the never-ending fallibility of the created!

The one group of people who should be the stabilizing factor for the entire world is the church. But all over the world, we sit by passively and agree with a logic that allowed liquor stores to stay open and churches to be closed! We yielded to medical advice that was neither medical nor biblical. We closed the doors to our churches without a word of protest.

My goal is not to shame the church; my goal is to wake up the church! If we do not stand up and use our influence for good, we are complicit in the rise of evil! No one in the world has access to the solutions we have. But we have grown to trust the government more than the Word of God. But a new day is coming!

15

THE BEGINNING OF SORROWS

Jesus said something very interesting about this time of turmoil. First, He said, *this is not the end!* Then, He described it as *the beginning of sorrows.*

As mentioned earlier, the end, as used here, is not talking about the end of time. Strong's Concordance defines it as: *to set out for a definite point or goal; properly, the point aimed at as a limit.*[6] This can still be a little vague until we pair it with the word sorrows.

Sorrows refer to birth pangs, i.e., the pain a mother endures to bring a new life into the world. The *e*nd refers to a specific goal, deliberately sought. All of the fabricated tragedies befalling the planet are the consequence of a plan and purpose: The purpose is to usher in a New World Order, a global society that rejects all the values, ethics, and morals provided as a basis for civil order and justice. This an era of unprecedented lawlessness (iniquity)!

The mystery of iniquity (lawlessness) has existed in the world since the serpent showed up in the Garden of Eden (2 Thessalonians 2:7). Lawlessness is rejecting God's commandments for justice, civil order, and love and replacing them with humanistic philosophies.

---

6   Biblesoft's New Exhaustive Strong's Numbers and Concordance with Expanded Greek-Hebrew Dictionary. Copyright © 1994, 2003, 2006 Biblesoft, Inc. and International Bible Translators, Inc.

True luciferianism is based on the angry God doctrine. Luciferians promote the idea that God is angry and only seeks to control and suppress the human race. They encourage the religious distortion of sovereignty, which violates everything God says about man's authority on planet Earth.

Sovereignty is redefined: instead of freedom to act independently, it is changed to mean absolute control. The deception is this: God is in control of everything. Therefore, everything bad that happens is God's fault. If God is love, there would be no wars, famine, crime, suffering, or pain in this world. After all, He is in control! This false concept of sovereignty has probably caused more people to hate God than anything religion has ever concocted! Every bad thing in the world is blamed on God!

God created man in His *likeness and image* and gave him authority over planet Earth. This should be one of the most faith-building, hope-inspiring realities in the Bible. Based on this, every person can be who he or she chooses to be. Every person can trust God, believe His promises, and act with authority for his outcome. Others can affect our lives, but no one can control them!

Sadly, this is possibly one of the most disbelieved, rejected, and despised truths in God's Word. Why? It makes man responsible. The book of Proverbs provides a fascinating insight into the extremes to which man will go to avoid responsibility, *"A man's foolishness destroys his life, but in his heart, he blames God."* Proverbs 19:3 It seems the human race would rather blame God for a bad experience than consider the possibility that our choices may be the problem.

Psalm 82 is a dialog in which God explains to the human race that they have free will to rule the world as they choose. If they judge fairly, there will be justice; if there is no justice, it is because they rejected His justice. Read and reflect on God's questions and instructions to those who rule. Psalm 82:

2. How long will you judge unjustly, And show partiality to the wicked?

3. Defend the poor and fatherless; Do justice to the afflicted and needy.

4. Deliver the poor and needy; Free them from the hand of the wicked.

5. They do not know, nor do they understand; They walk about in darkness; All the foundations of the earth are unstable.

6. I said, "You are gods, And all of you are children of the Most High.

7. But you shall die like men, And fall like one of the princes."

Man, not God, chooses to bring chaos or peace, justice, or lawlessness to the world. It happens based on who and what we trust. Do we trust greed-driven politicians or the eternal God? Do we put our hope in man's contrived theories or the wisdom of God expressed in His eternal Word? Do we believe man is more fair and just than our Creator? That is the statement we make every time we allow a law to be passed that takes away our religious freedoms or opposes the commandments of God!

The Biblical concept of a curse is when people make choices, despite God's warnings, and receive the consequences of the decision. All these things, Jesus warned us to rise above, lead to what comes next. The horrors are not the wrath of an angry God; they are the consequences of evil, power-hungry, greedy people, and a complacent, compromised church. But it is not too late!

Shaming the church is not my intention; I intend to awaken the church to our God-ordained place of godly influence. We have the wisdom of God's Word; we can bring justice to the world!

16

GIVING BIRTH TO WHAT?

As we have discovered, all the things Jesus warned of would come, if we give way to deception, are birth pangs. These birth pangs are the strategy of social upheaval, designed to usher us into a world without God! Birth is given to a New World Order, controlled by the elite. According to Jesus, here's what it will look like:

> *Then they will deliver you up to tribulation and kill you, and you will be hated by all nations for My name's sake. And then many will be offended, will betray one another, and will hate one another. Then many false prophets will rise up and deceive many. And because lawlessness will abound, the love of many will grow cold. But he who endures to the end shall be saved. And this gospel of the kingdom will be preached in all the world as a witness to all the nations, and then the end will come.*

> Matthew 24: 9-13

A world without God means an amoral world. Corruption replaces work ethic, people succeed, not because they work hard and are honest, but because they are shrewd and ruthless. One of the primary things that disappear in the New World Order is love for one another. Love is value; in the NOW, love is a weakness. Serving others is not an admirable goal for the elite. Their goal is to have others serve them!

The only way to eradicate the knowledge of God from the earth is to eliminate the people who know God. Christians and Jews will be accused of every evil thing imaginable. The compromised church will justify cowardice by readily believing the accusations. Just as it was with the rise of Hitler, the churches that align with State policy and guidelines will be allowed to continue. What those churches fail to understand is they will only be allowed to exist until they have served their purpose!

I know the average believer refuses to accept this reality, which means they do not believe the words of Jesus. These things are already happening in the world. According to an article in Christianity Today, right now in China, the government is sweeping through provinces. All Christians receiving any kind of state assistance must surrender their Bibles, get rid of all Christian paraphernalia, denounce Jesus as Lord and acknowledge the head of the Communist party as Lord.

Within my congregation, I have witnessed career military personnel forced out because they refused to denounce Jesus as Lord. This didn't happen yesterday; this occurred in the 1980s and 1990s. This has been happening covertly in America for decades.

> We refuse to see that the socialists and elitists are the ones who want to pattern our government after China.

I know you still think this could never happen in America. We refuse to see that the socialists and elitists are the ones who want to pattern our government after China. They are the ones who have made hidden trade deals with China that have robbed our country of jobs while attempting to crash our economy. They are the globalists who want a One-World government. They are the ones who took prayer out of schools and removed all biblical quotes from government buildings. They passed laws protecting murderers, rapists, and thieves while doing nothing for law-abiding citizens. They are the ones inciting riots and chaos in the streets. In the name of fairness, they allow the lawless to burn houses and businesses of honest, hard-working people. Under the guise of compassion, they release murderers and violent offenders from prison, sending them back to terrorize the same neighborhoods where they committed their crimes! These are the same people who protest and make speeches when police kill a criminal in the act of committing a crime, but never raise their voice for the babies, children, preteens, and other innocents shot down for nothing more than the joy of murder!

The beginning of sorrows, i.e., birth pangs, delivers us into The New World Order, an elitist society controlled by a One-World government! We can stop this downward spiral now, but once the baby is born, it will be too late!

It would be easy to think this is about political parties and treat this like it has nothing to do with God or faith, but nothing is farther from the truth! The first commission given to man from God, was to rule and reign. We were to maintain God's justice in the world. Today's injustice is a combination of what the evil makes happen, and what the fearful and unbelieving allow to happen!

The facts are undeniable; the track record of the socialists and globalists prove their promises are gross lies; they are deceitful tactics to destroy the world as we know it and remake it in their likeness and image. Their version of justice is: "We, the elites, are the only ones worthy of the world's resources. The inferior must comply with our demands or face elimination." Since all the facts are apparent, why doesn't everyone see it?

17

WHAT YOU SEE ISN'T ALWAYS WHAT YOU PERCEIVE

After nearly a half-century of counseling and consulting, I have discovered that few people distinguish the difference between what they see and what they perceive. We see with our eyes, but what we see transforms into what is perceived by our brain! Our brain interprets facts, based on our beliefs and judgments, literally reshaping what we see and hear!

So many times, when someone who has been offended describes what they saw or heard, their description is not based on reality; it is a delusion. A delusion is an internal distortion that either denies facts or is the product of external deception. In either case, it means they are experiencing pain and suffering caused by an imaginary perception of an event, not the event itself! The incident may have happened, but it never actually happened the way it was experienced.

The Bible calls on every believer to question the source of their hurt. Did this happen the way I remember and experience it, or do my judgments alter my memories and experience? Very few are willing to consider their role in their pain! People are programmed to think like victims. A victim mentality refuses to accept responsibility for pain. They are programmed to look for someone to blame! The first step toward resolving an offense is to determine if it is self-inflicted or the intentional actions of others!

In Matthew 7, Jesus warns about the self-inflicted pain of judgment.[7] Judgment occurs when we attempt to determine good or bad intentions in a person's behavior. In other words, we try to judge why someone said or did something. Once we determine why a person did something, we have given significance to their actions. The problem is that the pain we feel is more the consequence of our judgments than their actions.

In Matthew 7:2, Jesus explained, *"With the measure you use (apply), it will be measured back to you. "* He further explains that when you assume to know why someone did what they did, you are presuming to know the intention of their heart. You are attempting to see what is known by God alone! You can indeed identify what someone does. It is, however, impossible to know why.

We manufacture self-inflicted pain by delusional thinking. The Bible calls it judging. When I assume that you did something for a hurtful reason, I experience the pain of a deliberate harmful action. When I pass no judgment concerning why you did something, it alters the effect.

> We manufacture self-inflicted pain by delusional thinking. The Bible calls it judging.

The power of judgments reveals the desperate need for such intensive propaganda by the media, educators, and political and religious leaders. In order to inflame an entire race, there must first be widespread miseducation. Explosive reaction to racism is rarely ever racism; it is usually a judgment passed about the actions of another. The person passing the judgment is more morally culpable than the person who committed a racially insensitive act!

If you are a minority and you think all whites are racist, you will be continuously offended by the actions of others. It will not be their behavior that is offensive and hurtful; it will be the judgments you pass about their behavior. You will create an incurable scenario, based on delusion, rather than fact!

The Bible teaches us to consider the feelings of others; it's called walking in love. But when anyone can claim offense at a statue, flag, bumper sticker, cotton balls, and the like, and further accuse someone of racism because they don't share their outrage, it implies social insanity. Their selfish insensitivity would be a sin, in God's eyes, far worse than the racism they accuse. It would indicate an infringement upon a role belonging only to God: judgment!

Some would say, if you're walking love, you will always be sensitive to others. However, that which offends is subjective. There is no way one can know what offends another unless they are told. Being told is not synonymous with being attacked or threatened. The Bible says love is not easily offended. The easily offended are conditioned to be codependent victims. They have no intention to walk in love, but they insist everyone else should walk in love. Like all who share the victim's mentality, they place the responsibility for their happiness, unhappiness, poverty, or other undesirable conditions on others. They assume little or no responsibility for their actions or reactions!

> God has compassion for every person who suffers, even those who suffer from their own decisions.

God has compassion for every person who suffers, even those who suffer from their own decisions. But the one consistent theme of God's Word is personal responsibility. Our ability to change the quality of our lives by our choices may be the most definitive evidence that we are created in the likeness and image of God. Any religion, political system, or human philosophy that wants to make the decisions to give you a better life is subtly undermining your faith in your Creator and your identity as a child of God!

We are looking at the world through a lens created by anti-God elitists who have shaped our education, entertainment, morals, and values. When we look at the world through God's Word as Jesus taught, interpreted, and applied, we can free ourselves from the illusion of powerless codependency projected on us and step into our true identity!

There will never be a world without racism, hatred, greed, or murder beyond the degree that people become disciples of Jesus and walk in love. Every believer, especially every leader, should know, freedom, peace, joy, and all other healthy desires of life do not come to us based on what others do, say, or believe. They come to us when we believe God's truth in our hearts.

The offender made whole by the love of God stops offending. The offended made whole by the love of God stops being easily offended. The church is the only entity capable of bringing God's love to the world. If it is not manifesting, we are the ones who must step up, believe it, seek it, preach it, and model it.

18

The Mystery of Lawlessness

The Bible distinguishes the character of Jesus in a juxtaposition of lawlessness and righteousness. Jesus didn't just love righteousness; He hated lawlessness!

"Your throne, O God, is forever and ever; A scepter of righteousness is the scepter of Your kingdom. You have loved righteousness and hated lawlessness." Hebrews 1:8-9

Righteousness and lawlessness are the two opposing spiritual mindsets! The Kingdom of God is governed by righteousness; the World's System by lawlessness (iniquity). Regardless of what we say or how we justify our actions, all of our decisions are in harmony with one of these two influences. There is no third influence! This is what Jesus meant when He said, *"He who is not with Me is against Me, and he who does not gather with Me scatters abroad."* Matthew 12:30 There is no in-between. We either turn people to God or away from God.

Everything Jesus taught and modeled was based on God's Word, motivated by love. Consequently, everything about His life and ministry was a demonstration of righteousness. The benefits that came into the lives of those to whom He ministered was the fruit of righteousness!

We seem to forget that Jesus lived and ministered in Rome, the evilest empire that existed up to that point. The religious leaders of His day had turned God's Word into a system of legalistic control and manipulation. They obtained their positions, both political and religious, by paying bribes to Roman officials. Because of religious and political oppression, and propaganda, Israelites blamed every bad event in their lives on God.

Yet, in this hostile environment, Jesus never promoted riots, violence, or rebellion. Likewise, the fruit of His teaching and preaching never led to those ungodly actions. Jesus was a peacemaker; *"The fruit of righteousness is sown in peace by those who make peace."* James 3:18 He taught believers to experience God in their hearts, not through the subjective interpretation of their circumstances.

Jesus' messages about Kingdom living shared several consistent themes. He wove the golden thread of personal responsibility into every parable. He did not encourage the path of lawlessness. He challenged every person to connect with God, experience His love and power, and to be the change they wanted to see. He explicitly stated that those who choose lawlessness do not intimately know Him, Matthew 7:23.

> The three primary components of righteousness are the God's Word, the motivation of love, and faith.

The three primary components of righteousness are the God's Word, the motivation of love, and faith. If any of these three elements are absent, it is no longer righteousness. God's Word, not motivated by love, is usually harsh and condemning. God's Word, not empowered by faith, will always devolve into religious, dead works! Faith not based on God's Word is wishful, delusional imagining. Remove any of these elements, and there is no righteousness!

Jesus made it clear that love is the element that binds all things together perfectly. However, He showed us that love creates a win-

73

win situation. He said, love God, love your neighbor, and love yourself, Matthew 22:37-40. The scriptural basis of interpretation and application of every word and action of God must *hang* on this truth! As believers, this must be our basis and motivation for all we do!

There are many who claim to be ministers of the gospel, approving or provoking lawlessness, rioting, and violence, in the name of Jesus. Jesus is the Prince of Peace, not the king of chaos. Doing something in the name of the Lord does not imply God has approved it, Matthew 7:21-22.

There seem to be three different types of lawlessness in the world, either intentional or ignorant! At the top of the political stack are the elitists; they are working a deliberate plan to remove all knowledge of God from the earth! I am not writing this book for those people. I am writing this book for the second group.

The second type of lawlessness is non-believers. The Socialist elitists have brainwashed non-believers. They are the product of their beliefs. They are in darkness and have never seen the light. All they know about God is what the church has shown them. Sadly, the church has failed to show the love of God to the world. Now in this time of tribulation, we have failed to show them the *way of peace*!

Then there are Christians who think sincerity is the only requisite for representing God. They assume that their desire to help makes their efforts kind and godly. They unintentionally reject God's wisdom for justice and replace it with theories and philosophies that reject His Word. I am not saying this is the action or position of all believers. But the part of the church that is being heard is

74

the part that Isaiah, the prophet, said caused people to blaspheme God continually (Isaiah 52:5 and Romans 2:24).

At the end of a long sermon, Jesus wrapped up His theme perfectly. In the first few verses of Matthew 5, Jesus juxtaposes the characteristics of those who yield to righteousness to those who yield to lawlessness. One represents those who live and abide in the Kingdom of God; the other represents those who live according to the world's system.

He explains, *"Do not think that I came to destroy the Law or the Prophets, I did not come to destroy but to fulfill."* Matthew 5:15 *"Fulfill"* does not mean "to do away with." He made that clear. *"Fulfill"* means to bring to complete perfection, to cause it to reach its intention.[8] Jesus showed and taught us that the law only fulfills God's objectives when applied by love.

In verse 26, Jesus explains that if you owe money and go to jail, you need to stay until you pay the debt. He's not here to deliver us from civil consequences. In other words, His love and grace do not nullify justice.

In the following verses, He makes it clear that He is here to do a work in our hearts! If we are unwilling to change what's in our hearts, the only remaining motivation to change our lifestyle is consequences.

As believers, we should inspire people to trust God, surrender their hearts to Jesus, and walk-in love. To encourage or support anything else means that we are workers of iniquity! No matter how sincere our intentions, we are complicit in leading people away from God, i.e., scattering!

---

8   Thayer's Greek Lexicon, Electronic Database. Copyright © 2000, 2003, 2006 by Biblesoft, Inc. All rights reserved.

Jesus wraps up the sermon in Matthew 7:21-23 when He says,

> *Not everyone who says to Me, "Lord, Lord," shall enter the kingdom of heaven, but he who does the will of My Father in heaven. Many will say to Me in that day, "Lord, Lord, have we not prophesied in Your name, cast out demons in Your name, and done many wonders in Your name?" And then I will declare to them, "I never knew you; depart from Me, you who practice lawlessness!"*

It doesn't matter if Jesus' name is on our lips or the sign in front of our church. If we are promoters of lawlessness, we have no intimate involvement with Him. We are not for Him, we are against Him. We are not gathering people to God. We are driving people away from God! We are not delivering people from bondage. We are ushering them into bondage!

It is time to lay down our special-interests and follow the one commission He gave us: to be and make disciples.

It is time for every believer, especially every leader, to awaken unto righteousness! It is time to lay down our special-interests and follow the one commission He gave us: to be and make disciples. Teach and model how to live a life in harmony with God!

To understand the mystery of lawlessness and how we got here, we must correctly define both iniquity and mystery! We already clearly explained lawlessness: rejecting God's laws and commandments as the only standard of ethics, morality, love, and justice!

A mystery, according to the Bible, is something hidden that is revealed by initiation. The degree we thoroughly accept what we learn at our current level of initiation, we move forward to an initiation into a deeper level. Cults use this as a form of brainwashing. They never reveal their true intentions until you are fully indoctrinated.

The intention of this book is not to discuss the ultimate outcome of lawlessness. I must, however, mention that once the world loses the knowledge of God's justice, it will fall into such chaos that it will reach a place of no return. We, the believers of the world, can awaken to righteousness, stand up and postpone that which looms of the horizon. We hold the fate of billions in our hands. This book is a call to save our generation, our children, our nation, and the world!

For the Christian, lawlessness is a mindset we slowly and incrementally accept until it changes the way we perceive and understand God and His Word. This usually begins with compassion, and a heartfelt desire to help others, defined by humanistic philosophies! But it ends by not only destroying the people we set out to help; it destroys us and all we love!

THE POWER OF GODLY INFLUENCE

The great seduction destroying our world is the Mystery of Iniquity, cloaked in the promise of a fair, just world of love and peace. The last 70 years of indoctrination into relativism has made us susceptible to the destructive logic that the end justifies the means!

The truth, however, reveals that the means don't justify the end; they're just a preview of the end! The means being employed to create a fair and just utopian society expose the lie. There is an important biblical principle called the *law of the seed!* This is an irrefutable law governing all things spiritual, physical, emotional, and relational. Jesus taught that failing to accept the law of the seed would make it impossible to understand any of the parables of the Kingdom (Mark 4:13)!

Although there are many subtleties, the law of the seed starts with one simple reality; the seed you plant determines the fruit. The seed of deceit cannot bring forth the fruit of honesty; injustice cannot produce justice; wrath and violence cannot make a peaceful world. A second ignored dynamic of the seed is, one seed always produces many more seeds of its own kind. Therefore, as Jesus said that if you don't plant new seeds, you get more of what you've got! The violence that brings forth the New World Order means violence will multiply exponentially once it starts to bear fruit!

We have lost touch with the fact that God's nature, the one thing that motivates all His commandments and actions, is a love so deep and pure there are no words to describe it. There is no deceit in anything God says or does; there is no unrighteousness! His warnings are not the intimidation of wrath as punishment; they are to enlighten us to the danger, allowing us to choose a different path!

> There is no deceit in anything God says or does; there is no unrighteousness!

God was in the process of delivering the Children of Israel from the idolatrous nation of Egypt. Much like God is trying to deliver us from the grips of an evil and lawless world! Had the Israelites trusted and obeyed God's wisdom, they could have arrived in Canaan in eleven days. Instead, they wandered in the wilderness for forty years! This reveals another amazing secret: righteousness can bring us into the promises of God much faster than we have imagined!

The theme of the book of Exodus is: *Be holy because I am holy.* Contrary to centuries of religious dogma, the underlying meaning of *holy* is to be *uncommon*. God was unlike any of the gods in Egypt. He was not common! The pagan gods were wrathful. People made sacrifices as a means to garner favor and escape the wrath of their gods. God was not like any of those gods! God is love!

Sadly, the Israelites did what he warned them not to do. They interpreted His commandments, feasts, and sacrifices based on what they believed about other gods. All the hardships that befell them occurred because they refused to believe His promises and apply the wisdom of His Word, independent of personal religious interpretation!

Moses was already struggling with the unbelief and hard-heartedness of the Israelites, which would have disqualified him from leading them into the Promised Land. But God was about to deliver the most compassionate, liberating, moral code ever heard in the ancient world. God could not risk misrepresentation by His chosen leader.

The nations of the world would see God manifest in the people who lived by this code!

This was the code of social justice that became known as the Law and the Commandments! It would take volumes to explain all the freedoms given to the nation of Israel that were previously never applied in any society. It would be this code of social justice that would be so radically different. It would reveal the character and nature of the Creator to the world. The nations of the world would see God manifest in the people who lived by this code!

Unfortunately, the Israelites did not believe or apply the Law the way God presented it. They turned it into a fear-based means of judging and controlling others. God did not give the law as a means of making anyone righteous. It was a way for a person to identify if they were walking in love, i.e., treating others with respect! It was an outward description of how we would treat one another when love is in our hearts.

God told the Israelites to be like Him. The commandments God gives man are the same injunctions He observes in relating to man. Unlike the pagan gods, there wasn't one code of justice for God and a higher code of justice for the worshipper!

Moses was about to receive what should be the most liberating code of social justice ever given. If he misinterpreted or misapplied it, man would be no better. Before Moses could lead as God would lead, he had to have something change in his heart!.

Moses requested to see God's glory (Exodus, 33:18). I have to wonder what Moses expected to see, and what did he hope it would do for him? When a king would show his glory, it would usually come down to a display of power! Did Moses expect to see God's power in a way that would give him the courage to lead these difficult, rebellious people? I don't know, but I'm reasonably sure Moses did not see what he expected.

God's response to Moses' request almost seems as if God wasn't listening. However, God is a heart-God! He hears our words but responds to the cry of our hearts. Sometimes words reflect what we think we should say when our heart is crying for something far more relevant!

Just a few days earlier, Moses made another request, *"I want to know your ways."* Exodus 33:13 Moses knew he needed something, but like many believers, he assumed to know what he needed to experience to know God's ways! So he proceeds to request to see God's glory. As always, God looked past the limitations of Moses' word and answered the cry to his heart!

The primary distinction between Moses and the rest of the Israelites was that they were content to see his deed, but Moses wanted to understand His ways. Twenty-first century Christians may cry out for God to fix problems, but the leaven of iniquity makes them believe there is a path to God's deeds other than walking in His ways. Only the applications of God's ways will end this present global destruction!

God's response to the request was, *"I will make all My goodness pass before you, and I will proclaim the name of the Lord before you."* Exodus 33:19. If God had been common, i.e., like the gods of Egypt, He would have displayed something to provoke fear and terror. Instead, He revealed His goodness. God has always been a "faith God," and faith works because we know His every action is motivated by love. We only trust God to the degree that we believe His goodness!

Religion has influenced us to believe the most significant manifestation of God's power is judgment. However, when we enter the epicenter of God's power (the holy of holies), we don't discover a judgment-seat; we find the mercy seat. James wrote, "*Mercy triumphs over judgment*" (2:13). It is the goodness of God that leads to repentance, not the wrath of God! No one is qualified to lead God's people until His goodness becomes the power of their influence!

20

THE PROCESS AND THE PROMISE

It's not enough to get people into a Promised Land; they must have the character to live and sustain the promise. The process employed to get something is the same process one must continue to maintain it. Violence and corruption can never lead to utopian peace and justice. Based on the law of the seed, it serves only to multiply and magnify violence and corruption.

If you notice, socialists, globalists, and anarchists never refer to America as a republic, only as a democracy. Through casual conversation, I've seen that few people know we are a republic. But what is even more frightening is very few people know the difference.

Jesus warned that our culture (our tradition) tends to make the God's Word *of no effect*. Americans have developed an interpretation of the Bible based on American culture. I have had thousands of conversations where Christians adamantly express beliefs about a particular social issue! When I ask, *"Where in the Bible did you get that belief?"* I am deeply saddened to hear the most common reply, *"I don't know; it's just what I believe!"*

American Christians not only think America is a democracy; subsequently, they believe the kingdom of God is a democracy. We seem to assume the laws that have preserved America are optional! It's the same with God's commandments; we assume we can change them just because our party presumes to be smarter than God! Even more absurd, we think God should or would answer prayers requesting Him to become a liar by blessing that which is rooted in lawlessness!

One of the most important concepts that you must learn if you desire to have heaven on earth, i.e., the Kingdom of Heaven, is that you must first surrender to Jesus as Lord and begin the journey of a disciple! The first characteristic required to start the journey of a disciple is to have a teachable repentant attitude.[9] God does not give up the wisdom of His Word; it is we who must give up our opinions and accept God's.

A set of laws rules a republic. In America, that set of laws is called the Constitution. No law can be legally passed by any city or state that violates the Constitution. The utmost responsibility of any elected official is to uphold and defend the Constitution. A democracy, on the other hand, is majority ruled. If both parties had not become so irresponsible concerning the Constitution, our country never could have devolved into this chaotic mess. Likewise, if the church had not become so lackadaisical about the need for God's justice, neither the church nor the country would be such a mess!

The framers of The American Constitution never intended for our country to become a pure democracy. Democracies always devolve into mob rule. People with money and power can always buy votes. Violent people terrorize citizens into voting a certain way. What is happening in America, and around the world, is mob rule by attempting to govern as democracies.

---

9   Dr. Jim Richards, Heaven on Earth, South Carolina, True Potential, 2018

The church has become mob rule. The Commandments, as Jesus taught them, is the believer's Constitution. Like the Children of Israel, instead of trusting God and walking in His ways, we have chosen our own. Since the church has chosen to ignore Jesus' commission to make disciples and has decided only to make converts, we have billions of people around the world who call themselves Christians, but do not know the ways of God!

This infectious mindset is the leaven working through and undermining our entire belief system, which has dummied us down to think that socialism is in harmony with God's will. We have become conspirators in preparing the world for the lawless one, the antichrist, who will seek to eradicate all knowledge of God from the earth! The way we have chosen is the seed of lawlessness, which will eventually give birth to a New World Order, based entirely on lawlessness!

If we desire a world of justice, we, like Moses, must cry out to know God's ways! We must read His Commandments, i.e., His rules for social justice, and we must never support those who reject them.

Since we are created in the likeness and image of God, ordained with authority on planet earth, we have the unique capability of harmonizing heaven and earth. We can choose and establish God's will on earth.

HARMONIZING HEAVEN AND EARTH

Religion has so twisted God's Word that socialism and other humanistic philosophies sound far more loving and compassionate than God's truth. Historically, however, socialism has always been a path to failed promises, corruption, and bondage. Additionally, it produced the same wrongs it promised to correct!

The seduction of socialism is at least threefold:

- It promises everything God promises.
- Up to a certain point is sounds just like God's Word.
- It sounds more compassionate than God's Word.

Confidence in God's compassion and love begins with believing He is good and only good. Moses' faith came to rest in God's goodness, after his experience on Mt Sinai.

Exodus 34:6 *"And the Lord passed before him and proclaimed, 'The Lord, the Lord God, merciful and gracious, longsuffering, and abounding in goodness and truth."*

In this passage, God now reveals four fundamental realities:

- He ensures He will only use His power for our good
- He explains why Moses experienced such a miraculous transformation.

- He connects His goodness to His name.

- He brings His name and character into congruent reality.

God starts by reminding Moses of two of God's core names: El & Jehovah.[10] According to some Hebrew scholars, El is more God's masculine name, revealing His power. Jehovah is more connected to the nurturing aspect of His nature, which He mentions twice. By expressing Himself as El, it could be God is saying, "Yes, I Am the Mighty One, the All-Powerful One." But then repeated Jehovah two times.

Knowing that God is all-powerful can invoke security or fear, until it is clear how He will use His power! Possibly He repeated Jehovah twice to ensure the primary use of His power is to nurture and protect.

Judaism breaks God's characteristics into thirteen attributes. I, however, see this as five attributes, then an explanation of how to apply these attributes in real-life situations.

Merciful: The Hebrew word used here is *Racham*. It is often translated as tender mercies, to have pity, to show compassion, or to love. However, *Racham*, according to Chaim Bentorah, my Hebrew teacher, actually speaks to a sweet, tender, interactive, relational love.[11] In application, this is referring to the tender, compassionate, understanding God gives to those who abide in a loving relationship with Him!

Gracious: It seems the word used here points to the fact God is prone to extend favor.

---

10   This is the English rendering. The Hebrews would never pronounce God's name. No one really knows how it was pronounced in ancient times.
11   Bentorah, Chaim. God's Love for Us: A Hebrew Teacher Explores the Heart of God through the Marriage Relationship (Kindle Location 1304 -1307). Kindle Edition.

Longsuffering: This emphasizes God's patience and how He is slow to anger.

Abounding in goodness: The Hebrew is *chesed,* pronounced *hesed.* In Michael Card's book, *Inexpressible: Hesed and the Mystery of God's Loving Kindness,* he explains how there is no word in any other language comparable to *hesed.* It is a word always used in conjunction with other adjectives expressing God's lovingkindness and goodness. I take this word to imply that God's goodness is beyond intellectual definition. Since it is used in connection with *racham,* it would seem to say that it can be experienced in an intimate relationship with God, even though it is beyond intellectual explanation!

Abounding in truth: The truth of God's Word is stability, among other things. This means genuine godly compassion is always guided by truth, no matter what emotions one may feel. The Hebrew letters used to spell truth implies that it is what makes it possible for man to come into harmony with God. It also indicates that truth is the only thing that can harmonize heaven and earth. We can only have the world God offers when we harmonize that world with God's truth, i.e., justice.

These attributes are the manifestation of God's name and the fruit they produce in our lives. If we believe in the name of the Lord, this is what we confidently expect in our every interaction with the Father. This is how we express ourselves to others! When Moses believed in the name of the Lord, as God defined it, he had an experience so overwhelming it altered his physical appearance and his moral character. More importantly, it changed how he led and influenced the Israelites. When we see God as He is, we, too, are transformed into that image, morally and ethically!

God gave man authority over planet Earth (Genesis 1:26). He gave us the responsibility to apply His justice to the world. Psalm 82 explains the reason for all the chaos on earth is our refusal to rule in harmony with God's justice!

God desires heaven on earth; it has always been His desire, and He has always attempted to lead us into that reality. When man surrenders to God, His will can be done on earth. Men will only rule in a way that expresses the character of God if their hearts have been transformed by surrendering to Jesus as Lord. Then and only then will the inhabitants of earth reflect the character and nature of God and experience true justice, i.e., heaven on earth!

Socialism and almost every other human philosophy offer heaven on earth, but without God's presence, there is no heaven. Where God's Word is rejected, God Himself is rejected!

Where God's Word is rejected, God Himself is rejected!

Socialism would explain compassion, very similarly to what God said to Moses, but it would never make God's Word the harmonizing factor. Carnal compassion is nothing more than, codependent, enabling pity! Without God's Word, justice becomes anything we feel, anything we declare it to be. Thus, we have a world that cannot find peace and will not establish justice!

This book is a wakeup call to the church. Let's be engaged in the world by living and modeling God's compassion. God has not called us to clean up drug addicts. He has called us to set them free. He has not called us to demoralize people with hand-outs, but to help sustain them while they learn how to provide for themselves.

22

COMPASSION THAT KILLS OR HEALS

Several times in His ministry, compassion moved Jesus to take action. Why? Compassion is part of the character and nature of God. He hurts when His children hurt! But Jesus' compassion never took Him away from the truth; it never compelled Him to justify chaos, destruction, or unloving behavior.

Compassion always moves one toward action. Character determines what kind of action. The action taken by Jesus was to bring the person into harmony with the character and nature of God through healing and deliverance. Even in His parables, He taught that compassion would inspire people to forgive one another. In other words, compassion always leads the godly to godly action; it never leads to codependent enablement.

In the following verses, God reveals the difference between compassion that heals and compassion that kills.

In Exodus 34:7, God explains how His compassion and mercy make Him willing and capable of forgiving any type of sin: *"Keeping mercy for thousands, forgiving iniquity and transgression and sin."*

Religion makes us believe God's righteousness drives Him to hate and kill the sinner. But God explicitly declares the opposite. *"'As I live,' says the Lord God, 'I have no pleasure in the death of the wicked, but that the wicked turn from his way and live.'"* Ezekiel 33:11

Socialism teaches that societal influences cause people to become who they are. Therefore, no one can be held accountable for their behavior. Up to a point, this is true. However, God's justice draws people to godly social behavior by walking in love. God's Word always has a redemptive promise; socialism has no guarantee of redemption or transformation! It leaves you in moral corruption offering nothing more than excuses!

In the following statements, we discover the place where socialism and many humanistic Christians depart from God's wisdom. After the definitive statements about God's desire to forgive He says *"... by no means clearing the guilty."* Exodus 34:7

When God makes this statement, it seems He contradicts everything He has previously said. Part of the misunderstanding is in the translation from Hebrew to English. Two things come to mind when I read this verse.

Modern Christians seem to have great difficulty separating social justice from spiritual justice.

Modern Christians seem to have great difficulty separating social justice from spiritual justice. To make them both the same makes it impossible to understand how to bring the love of God to the hurting world without enabling a wicked world!

As you will discover in the next segment, social justice is a system of directives designed to protect society. Spiritual justice is how to protect the individual for eternity! God is always willing to forgive personally, even though, for the sake of society, the person must pay for their violations.

So God is saying what Jesus taught more than 1,000 years later in Matthew Chapter 5: *I will forgive you; I will comfort you; I will empower you into a new quality of character, but you still have to pay the price to those you have wronged!*

Through the religious translation of the last part of verse seven, God appears to be vile, unloving, and unfair. Let's clear up the confusion. Most English translations read:

"Visiting the iniquity of the fathers upon the children and the children's children to the third and the fourth generation."

Three ways we know this cannot be a proper translation:

- Other scriptures say just the opposite: Jeremiah 31:29-30, Deuteronomy 24:16. In Ezekiel 18:2. God told the Israelites to stop repeating this saying; a person will be punished, judged, or come under a curse because of their ancestors' sins!

- This concept is incongruent with, thereby denying, any of the names of God.

- Jesus corrected this corrupt theology when people blamed a child being born blind on the sins of his parents.

The Hebrew word *po-ked*, translated *visit*, should be translated as *remembers*, or *take into account*. In *The Rational Bible*, commentary of Exodus, Dennis Prager, translates the passage like this:

When God looks at us, He remembers that most of our corrupt beliefs and behavior have been the influence of society.

"God remembers the iniquity of parents upon children and children's children, upon the third and fourth generations."[12] God is confirming the fact that society, especially parents, influences our beliefs, behavior, morals, and ethics. Socialism begins with a biblically-based logic but then departs to something that opposes God's wisdom, producing the opposite of the help people need.

When God looks at us, He remembers that most of our corrupt

beliefs and behavior have been the influence of society. It's like He is saying, *I know you didn't get this messed up by yourselves. I understand how you got here! Therefore, I am moved with compassion! I'm not going to kill you, as your wickedness deserves. I will make you a new creation. I will be your Father and you God; I will lead you into a new life.*

In every situation, we have freedom of choice. We can reject God's call to repentance, but He will continue to call out to our hearts. However, if we choose to continue to hurt others, we must face social justice to protect the innocent! Even though God loves us and has no desire to see us suffer, He will always allow us to get what we choose. If people choose a life without God, they have chosen an eternity without God. That is not God's punishment; it is their choice! As stated previously, the curse is not what God does to punish us! The curse comes when we reject God's loving, warnings, and promises, i.e., we get the thing we wanted, despite God's Word and His Spirit trying to lead in a better way!

God never stops pursuing His children. *"When we are unfaithful, He remains faithful."* 2 Timothy 2:13 He doesn't stop offering love, because we reject love. He doesn't withdraw leadership because we are unwilling to follow. In referring to the *name* of God, the Hebrew for name is *Shem*. The two letters that spell the root word are *SHIN* and *MEM*. Understanding the meanings of these letters will help us understand the unwavering harmony between His name and His character.

The Hebrew letter *MEM* has at least two significant factors. Here we will focus on the meaning of *MEM* that represents passion, like a fire that burns. This letter indicates that God burns with a passion for His children to know and believe He is as His name reveals. Likewise, our belief in His name and the name of Jesus should be an all-consuming passion.

The closed letter *MEM*, as used here, represents a private message God longs to bring to our hearts. God has two kinds of knowledge. The first is the open *MEM*, which represents the revealed knowledge of God through His Word. But the closed (private) *MEM* represents how He wants to lead, protect, and enrich your life by teaching you the application of His written Word.

God is consumed with personal passion and desire to teach everyone how to live in His every promise. Even when we are undeserving, His passion and love never waivers. His compassion always leads us in paths of love, faith, and righteousness! The compassion that heals always calls us to repentance and faith. Conversely, the compassion that kills justifies and makes excuses, leaving the individual without hope.

People don't need to change to earn God's love; people need to change to prevent destroying themselves and everything they love. Additionally, if we bring people to Jesus as Lord, they will come out of their destructive lifestyles. They will become a new creation! Why do we side with political correctness and socialism, leaving them in the squalor of a life without God!

THE JUSTICE OF GOD OR THE JUSTICE OF MAN

It is amazing that as our world has become more humanistic, politically correct, and fair, it has grown more violent, immoral, and out of control! Man's codes of civil justice have never produced a fairer, more merciful world. However, those driving the insanity have no regard for facts and statistics. They are driven by ideology, not results!

As the elitist ideology becomes a more tangible reality, we see no justice, reprisals, or compensation provided for those who are victims of injustice. Yet, crimes against the political elite call for the most severe punishment.

Simply question the movement, and you could face a loss of income, public humiliation, physical attack, or death! Innocent people lose their jobs, homes are destroyed, and neighborhoods burned to the ground. Anyone who raises their voice for the innocent is vilified as a racist or hater!

Evil is called good, and good is called evil. We saw it in the pandemic. Murderers, rapists, thieves, and violent criminals were released from prison to protect them from Covid19. Yet, swift and extreme punishment was enacted upon those who didn't observe the six-foot-rule, went to church, or attempted to protect their family or property!

In the New World Order, the strictest punishments will be for those who, in word, thought, or deed, challenge, or even question the elitist ideology! The goal of the Woke socialist justice system serves little help to those who value law and order, hold jobs, and pay taxes. The primary function of their justice system is domination!

The biblical concept of justice is rooted in the Hebrew word for judgment. Judgment is a fair and equitable verdict. It should favor or disfavor no one. It should be impartial. Deuteronomy16:19-20, says:

> *You shall not pervert justice; you shall not show partiality, nor take a bribe, for a bribe blinds the eyes of the wise and twists the words of the righteous. You shall follow what is altogether just, that you may live and inherit the land which the Lord your God is giving you.*

Justice is for our benefit. It makes our country safe and secure.

Verse 19 provides obvious instructions for justice. But verse 20 dispels the idea that justice is about earning from God. Justice is for our benefit. It makes our country safe and secure. Many times when explaining scriptures about justice and loving treatment of our fellow man, God says that justice is what makes a nation healthy and stable. A fair and just system assures that you will remain in your country! When a nation's judicial system is corrupt and unfair, there are internal and external threats. Remember, great nations are seldom destroyed from the outside. They are usually destroyed internally by discontented troublemakers! When good people cannot find justice, they become angry; after all, the first responsibility of government is to protect its citizens.

Protect the innocent and the weak: Love is the expression of value for others. Criminals have no value for others. When the government refuses to protect the innocent, they prove they do not care about the well-being of the innocent, thereby making themselves conspirators with the criminals. It signals their true intentions, as well as their lack of character and ethics.

Prevent future crime: Repeat offenders repeat their offenses because they can. The consequences of their crime were not enough to deter them.

The socialists insist that we must put more effort into education. While I agree, I also believe the first lesson they must learn is that crime doesn't pay. Reduced sentencing for good behavior, plea deals, and other approaches toward rehabilitation are not designed to help the criminal. They don't help the victim, and based on recidivism, they don't prevent crime. They do, however, benefit the ineffective court and prison system!

Instruct the perpetrator: The biblical concept of a fool is one who will not learn by instruction. If a person does not learn by instruction and warning, the only hope they have of ever leaving a life of crime is consequences (Proverbs 17:10 and 19:29).

Instruct the observer: Consequences for the criminal discourage the young and foolish from following in their ways. One of the most absurd practices of our judicial system is the treatment of youth offenders. Youth offenders know they will pay minimal consequences for severe crimes. They also know their records will be sealed, providing a cover for their expansion into adult crime. Our system makes them believe they will never face the consequences.

Provide restitution for the wronged: As you will see in the next chapter, the biblical model for justice includes restitution to the victim. Our court system is no longer about justice for the victim; it's about justice for the State. In socialism, people are not tried for crimes against humanity. They are tried for crimes against the

State. A murderer doesn't answer to the family of the victim; they answer to the State. That's why the State can let a murderer walk on a plea deal, release them from prison, or choose not to try them when it might be a difficult case. Nothing about the current system is about justice for citizens. If someone wrongs you or your family, the State doesn't make them pay restitution; you have to file a civil case.

Perpetrators occasionally pay court costs. The offended party loses money and time, which cannot be recovered. The cost to the perpetrators is so minimal they are seldom discouraged from a life of crime. On the rare occasion when the perpetrator is ordered to pay some type of restitution, all the court fees must first be satisfied. It could be years before the victim recovers a single dollar. Then, in many states, a probation officer can decide to write off the debt, with no consideration or notification to the victim!

Every word of God has a goal: to teach us how to walk in love toward one another.

Every word of God has a goal: to teach us how to walk in love toward one another. The New Testament word for love, *agape,* means: to have value, hold in high regard, consider precious. God's commandments tell us how to express value for one another.

Love seeks to give, serve, and bring benefit to others. This isn't a call to codependence. Codependents sacrifice in order to be valued. Their ultimate goal is to meet their own needs, not the needs of others. God's love looks to meet the needs of others in a way that is not crippling, humiliating, or enabling!

Selfishness is when we do things with no regard for the value (love) of others. Those who practice this are willing to hurt others emotionally, financially, and physically, for personal benefit. The Law and the Commandments identify selfish, anti-love behavior. Biblical justice provides prevention, protection, and restitution to prevent crime and protect the innocent.

According to Anton LaVey, founder of the American Satanist Church, the purest form of satanism is not bowing down to Satan; it is selfishness. Selfish people hurt others; they do not walk in God's love. It is the epitome of evil. Every aspect of the modern judicial system is based on anti-biblical principles. It encourages selfishness, i.e., satanism.

One of the most discouraging factors in this corrupt system is when I see misdirected Christians and pastors fighting against God's wisdom for justice. They think they are benefiting society, but are only make matters worse for everyone except the criminal.

24

THE PENALTY MUST MATCH THE OFFENSE

In recent years, one of the strategies for chaos is presented in much-needed sentencing reform. The left has been very active in passing unjust sentencing laws. As always, they create the problem, blame others, then use the resulting crisis as a way to corrupt justice even more!

The biblical justice system requires that the penalty must match the offense. One of the clearest laws for fair sentencing is also one of the scriptures most twisted and attacked by socialists and religionists!

"Eye for eye, tooth for tooth, hand for hand, foot for foot, burn for burn, wound for wound, stripe for stripe." Exodus 21:24-25 Religion has interpreted this as a call to vengeance. Wrong! This judicial commandment is a two-edged sword; it cuts both ways. It is protection for the violated, as well as the perpetrator. This law is saying the penalty and compensation must match the offense. The violated cannot unjustly punish the perpetrator, but the violated will receive fair and just compensation!

Criminals are driven by many twisted emotions and justifications, ranging from entitlement, greed, lust, and sometimes nothing more than laziness. When there are no consequences for a crime, the crime is, by default, rewarded. It enables the criminal while confirming the idea that crime does pay. In the absence of fair and just laws based on an eye for an eye, the criminal gets what they want. They steal, i.e., take what others earn. This is the very core of socialist equality. Steal from those who earn and give to those who do not!

If a person steals, it is because they don't want to work. God's justice forces them to develop the character they presently lack. In cases of theft or burglary, the perpetrator should always pay back double what they took or tried to take (Exodus 22: 7 and 9). In some cases, thieves pay back seven-times what they stole (Proverbs 7:30). If a person is too lazy to work, but they are made to repay what they stole plus a penalty, they learn a lesson. It's easier to work and earn money that it is to steal. Restitution is far more effective than imprisonment.

Today, our courts are bogged down with frivolous lawsuits. Under the biblical policy, if a person sues and loses, or tries to win by false witnesses, the accuser and the false witness must pay what they tried to get from the accused (Deuteronomy 19:16-21). Our current judicial system seems to exist to make money for lawyers more than any other reason.

I believe in peaceful protests; however, domestic terrorists infiltrate peaceful demonstrations. They are no different than the middle-eastern terrorists who send children out in front of their troops or hide weapons near schools and hospitals. If anyone fires at them, the lying media will accuse them of murdering children. If they destroy their weapons, there is a danger of hurting school children or the sick! The terrorists are willing to kill and injure their own children and fellow countrymen to accomplish their evil intentions!

Likewise, those who infiltrate peaceful protests are willing to endanger those with a just cause, as a means to rioting, murdering, and destroying property. Because of the corrupt media, any attempt to protect the innocent is reported as a violation of civil rights! The socialist-elitist media is always complicit in destroying those they claim to help!

The way to stop rioting is *an eye for an eye*. When someone burns down a house or business, they should pay to rebuild it. Whatever harm they do to anyone, they should have it done to them. This is not vengeance; this is justice. I can assure you, if people knew they would die for committing murder, the murder rate would instantly decrease.

Socialism says that it is cruel to make the criminal accountable for what they do to the innocent. We should understand the needs of the troubled, angry, or violent. We should do the opposite of what God's Word states; we should declare them innocent.

For decades the church, right along with the world, has accepted the principles of class and race propaganda. Consider this logic, people in poor neighborhoods commit crimes because they are poor. White people are racists because they are white. Those who have been hurt throughout life will become sociopaths, pedophiles, rapists.

The Christian who accepts this logic is altogether rejecting the redemptive power of our risen Lord! Today, this logic is peddled to pervert self-responsibility and justice. In the future, this logic will be justification for genocide. After all, if all unacceptable behavior is uncontrollable, the only cure will be disposal of the one demonstrating unacceptable behavior.

There is already a bogus theory floating around certain agencies of a gene that causes people to be religious fanatics. At some time in the future this could be the justification for the mass murder of Christians. After all, it has already been done to Jews.

For now, socialism says when the poor commit crimes, we should show leniency; they only steal because they are poor. Exodus 23:6, states, *"Judgment cannot be perverted simply because someone is poor."* Leviticus 19:15, explains that it is corrupt to give partiality to the rich or the poor. *"You shall do no injustice in judgment. You shall not be partial to the poor nor honor the person of the mighty."*

Colors, races, and classes are not what cause people to commit crimes. That which causes a person to commit crimes against another is the condition of their heart (Mark 7:22-23).

If whites mistreat blacks, we say that it is racism. The Bible says that it is an evil heart. If whites kill and rob blacks, why do they kill and rob whites? If killing blacks is proof of racism, more blacks are racists against their people than whites. After all, the number of black-on-black crime far outweighs white on black crime. The same whites who rob, rape, murder, and mistreat blacks, rob, rape, murder, and mistreat whites. Likewise, the same blacks who rob, rape, murder, and mistreat blacks do the same to whites. Evil hearts, void of the knowledge of God, do evil things!

Wake up, America! Wake up, church! Crime exists because of what is in a person's heart, and it is exacerbated by a social justice concept that rejects everything our Creator told us about justice! Church, teach people the truth of God's justice. Make disciples who will be empowered by God to a better quality of life. Stop being a conspirator in creating a victim's society!

25

Is Man More Righteous than God?

The book of Job is probably misquoted more than any book of the Bible. It's not that the Scriptures are misstated, but taken out of context. For thirty-seven chapters, Job and his friends seek to justify their opinions about why Job was facing such calamity. Amazingly, we quote their foolish, ungodly reasonings, but never actually repeat what God says!

Finally, in Chapter 38, God begins to speak. He unscrambles their illogical confusion, self-justification, and accusations, driving their arguments and opinions. God asks, *"Who is this who darkens counsel by words without knowledge?"* (Job 38:2). In other words, you guys are not making the knowledge of God clear; you are making it confusing and hard to understand by mixing in your opinions!

Then in Job 40:2, God asks, *"Shall the one who contends with the Almighty correct Him?"* Even though Job was a righteous man, he was still human, with the need to justify himself. We, like Job, would prefer to express our opinion rather than discover what God has said. In other words, we want to instruct God.

In this matter, Job's friends correctly assessed Job's self-justification, *"Do you think this is right? Do you say, 'My righteousness is more than God's?'"* Job 35:2 No one would say the words, *"I am more righteous and fair than God."* Yet, every time we accept any philosophy or system of justice differing from God's justice, we are declaring, *"I am more just and fair than You!"* Furthermore, every vote for a politician proposing laws in conflict with God's justice is a vote against God. It is a vote for lawlessness! We are contending with and instructing the Creator, instead of listening, learning, and correcting our course!

In Job 40:8, God asks one of the most critical questions, *"Would you indeed annul My judgment? Would you condemn Me that you may be justified?"* We pray ridiculous, unscriptural prayers, asking God for outcomes that are incongruent with our actions. We refuse to raise our kids in righteousness, then pray for their lives to come out good! We cast votes for politicians supporting unjust laws and pray for a better world. We refuse to rule our world based on God's justice and are somehow amazed at the riots, crime, murder, and anarchy! Yet, when it goes wrong, we blame God. We create ridiculous theological concepts that justify our ungodliness while blaming God!

Religion has tricked us into thinking that faith is what we do to get God to respond to us. It has become our magic wand, get out of jail free card! But faith is not what we do to get God to respond to us; faith is how we respond to what God has said and promised. Stop trying to believe for what God will do and consider believing you can and will do what God says to do!

The core of all we need to know about God is His goodness, expressed in Exodus 34.6-8. God's justice is an expression of His goodness. Our willingness to trust God is based on our belief about His goodness. If we believe He is good, we will trust Him personally, as well as His standards for justice.

Maybe it's time we admit what I'm sure was hard for Job to admit. *"You asked, 'Who is this who hides counsel without knowledge?'"*

When I take a stand in opposition to Your justice, I hide Your goodness from the world. I pervert Your justice!

Job continued, *"Therefore I have uttered what I did not understand, Things too wonderful for me, which I did not know."* Maybe we should admit, I am not smarter than God. My theories are the foolish ramblings of an ego-driven world. You are the Creator. You know the heart of man. You and You alone can transform the hearts of those given to violence and evil! There is no social program that can do what needs to be done in the world!

Job closed with the humbling confession *"I have heard of You by the hearing of the ear, But now my eye sees You."* Job 42: 5 Maybe we should examine our hearts to determine if we have a living, vibrant, interactive relationship with God, or if we only call ourselves "Christian," with no commitment to Lordship or discipleship!

Get real about how you relate to everything, but especially about those to whom you give the power to rule you and your nation! We are not fairer or wiser than God. No matter how good it sounds when anyone exalts their goodness and justice above God's, whether intentional or accidental, they are destroying the world through lawlessness. I will not be a co-conspirator.

26

GATHERING OR SCATTERING

When the church accepts its position in the world, it will be the most powerful, influential group in existence. Because of ignorance and compromise it has, for decades, elected those promoting lawlessness, creating racial conflict, destroying the economy, and clearing the pathway for the eventual rise of the antichrist. We were left on planet Earth to guide, protect, and lead humanity into the knowledge of God. Instead, we have betrayed God and the people we are called to serve.

Don't get me wrong; there are great churches and great pastors, doing everything possible to save our world. When I use the word "church," I am talking about those who call themselves Christian. Those who claim to represent God! Maybe it's time to eliminate the word Christian from our vocabulary. If you are not a believer and a disciple, maybe you should redefine your relationship with God.

Jesus warned of a time when people would kill His disciples claiming to do God a service (John 16: 2-3). He explains the problem; they do not intimately know Him or intimately know the Father.

Like Job, they will believe they have been fair and righteous while blaming God for what befalls the world, then there will be the great falling away! The power-hungry deceivers will create the problem, and then they will promise to solve the problem if you re-elect them! This is your opportunity to break the cycle of lies, broken promises, and more deception. You can choose to remove the blinders. All you have to do is compare the plans, strategies, and policies of those in power with biblical justice!

Look at what these policies have produced! In America, every city that has been ruled by socialist leaders has shown declines in every quality of life criterion. It's not that confusing. Jesus said you know a tree by its fruit! Call it what it is!

This book is for every believer in every nation of the world. It is also for every person who doesn't understand why the world is so unfair. American Christians believe that most of our founding fathers were Christians. That probably isn't correct. We think a simple verbal statement identifying someone as a Christian is the standard of excellence! Christian voters were duped, over and over again, thinking they are electing Christians, but the problems never get solved.

> Part of the problem is the fact that God never called us Christians. Outsiders called us Christians.

Part of the problem is the fact that God never called us Christians. Outsiders called us Christians. It was more as a criticism than a compliment! I don't even know what a person means when they call themselves a Christian. It could mean they go to church occasionally, believe in their version of God, or that they were born in America. God called us children, heirs, believers, and disciples. When a person uses this terminology, we can look at how they relate to God, manage their lives, and relate to others to see if their lives bear the fruit of their confession. Know the tree by its fruit!

We have elected many "Christians" who were globalists, elitists, and outright pagans. It's time we quit thinking like children. Read the Bible, and get to know God personally. Stop following the blind! Our window for stopping the overthrow of the world is closing.

Most of the American founders were probably Deists. Since we can't know anyone's heart, we violate God's Word by judging others. We judge that any person claiming to be a Christian is a disciple, a faithful follower of God, and qualified to lead! Consequently, any candidate claiming to be a Christian usually gets the church's vote. That hasn't worked out very well!

Despite the questionable beliefs of our Founders, they all agreed with the morals and ethics presented in the Bible. They unanimously agreed that Jesus' morals and ethics would be the foundation of the Republic! God's Word was one of the primary sources for our Justice System. They also shared another consensus: when biblical morality was no longer the core value of individual citizens, our nation would destroy itself! They shaped our Constitution to protect us from elitism. We need people in office who understand the real threat and can act in harmony with the Bible even if they are not Christians.

For the believer, an election should never be about a candidate or political party. It is always a referendum for God's justice versus lawlessness. Elections are not a party issue or a personality contest. There are wicked politicians on both sides of the aisle. The only way to know the tree is to look at its fruit. Know the voting record of the person for whom you vote. Make your decision based on harmony with God's morals, ethics, values, and justice. Deal with your own political biases. More than that, together, let's reveal God's justice to the world.

Here's a great irony: when Jesus returns, He will rule and reign on earth for a thousand years. He will show us how wonderful life could have been if we had applied His justice. We could have that now if the church would awaken to righteousness and use its godly influence! The system of justice used during Jesus' reign will be the Commandments, i.e., the one system the world and most of the church does not trust!

Sadly, after a thousand years of peace and prosperity, the wicked will attempt another rebellion. Why? They hate righteousness; they are greedy. They want power, but mostly they want to fulfill the lusts of their flesh with absolute exemption from accountability to God! That's what they'll want then, and make no mistake, that's what they want now... a world without God!

Too many Christians feel they have the freedom to pick their candidate, vote with their party, or trust their opinions without acknowledging God! It's almost as if we think Jesus was incorrect when He said, *"He who is not with Me is against Me, and he who does not gather with Me scatters abroad."* Matthew 12:30 When we vote for politicians who reject God's Word and wisdom, we are scattering. We are creating the destruction of the world for which most will blame God. Our vote is more about whether we are for or against God, than whether we are for or against a particular candidate.

This book is for Christians who desire to become disciples, building their lives on the teachings of Jesus. Regardless of what happens next, knowing what you now know will preserve your life. Understanding God's justice will prevent us from making evil alliances, trusting the wrong people, and giving power to the wicked!

I know much of this has been challenging. Please don't take my word for any of this. Search Scripture for yourself. Open your heart fully to God, and together, we will create a fair and just world!

About the Author

In 1972, Dr. James B. Richards accepted Christ and answered the call to ministry. His dramatic conversion and passion for helping hurting people launched him onto the streets of Huntsville, Alabama. Early on in his  mission to reach teenagers and drug abusers, his ministry quickly grew into a home church that eventually led to the birth of Impact Ministries.

With doctorates in theology, human behavior and alternative medicine, and an honorary doctorate in world evangelism, Jim has received certified training as a detox specialist and drug counselor. His uncompromising, yet positive, approach to the gospel strengthens, instructs and challenges people to new levels of victory, power, and service. Jim's extensive experience in working with substance abuse, codependency, and other social/emotional issues has led him to pioneer effective, creative, Bible-based approaches to ministry that meet the needs of today's world.

Most importantly, Jim believes that people need to be made whole be experiencing God's unconditional love. His messages are simple, practical, and powerful. His passion is to change the way the world sees God so that people can experience a relationship with Him through Jesus.

To learn more about Dr. Jim Richards and Impact Ministires visit: https://impactministries.com/

Share this important message with your family, friends, church and community.

Use your smartphone camera on the flowcode images below to share *God's Wisdom for a Fair and Just World* on Social Media!

Share on Facebook   Share on Twitter

To purchase a print version of *God's Wisdom for a Fair and Just World* and for bulk discounts on the printed book, visit: https://www.truepotentialmedia.com/product/gods-wisdom-for-a-fair-and-just-world/
or use your smartphone camera on the flowcode image below to download a free copy or to purchase print a print copy of *God's Wisdom for a Fair and Just World*